4·2·99

Ask Nicky...

A Young Person's Workbook for Building Dreams

Dear Grandmother,
Your such a great inspiration to me & if anyone knows me it do grandma.

Written by Nicole Taylor and Frances Mejia Caldwell

This book is for you its Origonal your origanol im origanol wer the same Horiscope aquirious we have alot in common. Remember no one can ever take grandmothers place!

AYWN Publications and Training
Portland, Oregon

© 1999 Nicole Taylor and Frances Caldwell

All rights reserved. No part of this book, *Ask Nicky. . . A Young Person's Workbook for Building Dreams,* may be reproduced, stored in a retrieval system or transmitted in any form, or by any means, electronic, mechanical, photocopying, recording, or otherwise, without prior permission of the publisher.

Printed and bound in the United States of America

Book design and publication by AYWN Publications, 2711 NW St. Helen's Road, Portland, OR, 97210, phone: (503)222-6469, toll-free 1-877-262-5609, fax: (503)227-7470,
email: books@aywnpublications.com.

First edition

ISBN: 1-893471-01-2

This book is dedicated
to the thousands of young people all over the nation
who have died in violence in our cities' streets,
their potential and their dreams lost in one careless action.
May we never forget them as we strive everyday to live in peace.

Ask Nicky . . .

Table of Contents

Letter from Nicky *1*

1 What is a Gang? *3*
    Nicky's "Sweet Sixteen" Birthday Party *3*
    Alcohol and Other Drugs at a Party *7*
    Nicky Talks About Why Kids Join Gangs *7*

2 Friends: Love Them or Leave Them *11*
    Nicky Talks About Friendship *11*
    Who Can Be Trusted? *13*
    Nicky's Friend Sleepy *13*
    Handling Peer Pressure *16*

3 The Meaning of Family *19*
    Nicky's Mom's Story *19*
    Parents Aren't Perfect *21*
    Nicky's Letter to her Grandma *22*
    Family Squabbles *24*
    Role-Play a Negotiation *25*
    Nicky's Mom has Become her Best Friend *26*

4 Another View of School *29*
    Teachers Are People, Too *32*
    What is Education Anyway? *34*
    Be in Charge of Your Own Education *35*

5 Looking for a Role Model *39*
    Nicky's Positive Role Model *40*
    Who's a Positive Role Model? *42*
    Some Famous Positive Role Models *44*

Negative Role Models 44
You Are a Role Model 45

6 You--A Miracle in the Middle of Happening 47
   Self-Esteem 47
   Here's How Nicky Learned to Maintain Self-Esteem 48
   Self-Esteem is a Two-way Street 49
   Getting back to YOU 50
   Handling Criticism 51
   Bobbie G Learned to Love Himself Too Late 52

7 Pain: Yours, Mine, Ours 57
   "Taking Heat" 58
   Going to Jail 60
   Get Tough! 61
   Pain Can Be Contagious 63
   Nicky's Method 64

8 Peace. . . It Starts With You 67
   Nicky Writes About "Getting Out " 68
   Walk on the Side of Peace 70
   Behavior Chart 71
   Nicky Says, "It's Better to Walk in Peace than 'Rest in Peace'" .72

9 Dreams Give You Wings 75
   Dreams Can Come True 76
   Small Steps to Major Leaps 77
   Good Qualities and Skills to Hang a Dream On 79
   Things in Your Life You Want to Change 80
   Dreams May Change Over Time--Don't Fret 81
   Research on People Who Fulfill Their Dreams 82
   Nicky has a Dream. 83
   You have a Dream, too 85
   Special Thanks from Nicky 88

December, 1998

Hello, my name is Nicky.

This book is for you, written especially for you. I hope that my experiences will help you understand the truth about gang life. I hope you will be able to find a way to live your life that will bring you peace and success. I know from personal experience that living a life of violence will only bring you unhappiness and maybe worse, the end of a friend's life or your own. I'd like to be your friend.

I was born and raised in inner city North/Northeast Portland, Oregon. Because there was so much drinking and drug use in our home, my dad thought he could better himself and his family if he left. He didn't go far away, living in the same neighborhood; sometimes it feels to me like he never left. I was his first girl and only girl for a long time, although when I was five, my mom gave birth to a little girl named Tiesha, who died from crib death when she was six months old.

When my dad left, the family was made up of my mom, my five-year-old brother Terrance, whom we've always called Slim, and me; but my mom was pregnant with my little brother Sir Lawson, nicknamed Boomer, born six months later. While my mom was a single parent, I never downgraded her or blamed her for our being raised without our real daddy. I stayed by her side no matter what. I often talked to my dad over the phone and sometimes stayed nights with him and his new family. I love my stepmother. She never tried to keep me from seeing my dad and always wanted me over for visits. I now have two stepsisters. I love them the way I would a full sister.

Nonetheless, when I turned 13, I felt alone. My mom was always working, and I didn't have my dad when I wanted him because he lived with his other family. I wandered off to find a family in the streets. Before long, I was selling marijuana. I never told my mom where the money came from when she would find a bundle of money under my pillow or the mattress. At that age I never worried about the consequences.

My best friend Tinker and I were very popular in Portsmouth Middle School, and again when I reached high school, but then it was in a very negative way. On my sixteenth birthday, my auntie threw me a big "Sweet 16" party. I invited all my friends. That memorable night marked the beginning of my gang involvement and changed my life forever.

The stories in this book are all true, and each one has placed a scar on my spirit that is still painful to touch. I thank God, my grandmother, and my mother that I am alive and able to write these stories. I hope you can learn something from them.

Love
Nicky

1
What is a Gang?

> *A gang is a group of people who come together with a common cause or purpose. A group of people who work together to achieve a common goal can accomplish great and wonderful things, or they can immeasurably harm themselves and the people around them. Whether they work for good or for evil, they can wield tremendous power.*

Think about the definition given above. Based on this definition, can you name some gangs in our society? Have they helped or hurt other people? How? Why would someone want to join a group that caused hurtful things to happen?

When she was 16 years old, Nicky joined a harmful group whose main purpose was to hurt other people by selling them drugs, beating them up, or shooting at them or the people they cared about. The group she joined was the gang known as the Bloods.

It all began at Nicky's 16th birthday party. Nicky tells about a night in 1987 that she will always remember.

Nicky's "Sweet Sixteen" Birthday Party

My "Sweet Sixteen" birthday party on October 28, 1987, just two days before Halloween, looked like a complete success. A "Happy Birthday" banner was strung across my auntie's living room with orange and black *streamers woven over and under it. Balloons of every color bounced in all the corners and from the center light fixture. Beneath the decorations, a mass of bodies, teenagers mostly, swayed together to the beat of the pounding rap of Keith Sweat and Heavy D. Even my mom and her boyfriend were dancing, and my two aunties were helping guests serve themselves chicken, chips and dips, cake, orange sherbet punch, and strawberry daiquiris (without the alcohol). A huge sheet cake, now almost gone, celebrated three of us who were having birthdays that week-- Red Dog had just turned 18; my friend Tee Time Tangy who, like me, was just turning 16; and me.* This birthday bash fulfilled my auntie's promise to me, made two years earlier. I had wanted my sixteenth birthday party to be something I'd remember forever— something very special. It was, and I'll always remember it, but always with sadness.*

1990 Polaroid of Nicky and her homies

I had invited all of my friends; about 40 were expected. But you know how parties happen. Word gets around. I counted 125 around 10 p.m.

In 1987, nobody was worried much about gangs. We knew gangs existed; many of my friends were members, but no one had ever been shot. Sure, there was conflict between Bloods and Crips, but mostly it was talk. I had invited both Bloods and Crips because I had friends in both, and I thought they all respected my auntie and me too much to make a scene at my party. But the day of the party and well into it, a headache tormented me. My inner self was saying, "No, don't do this; don't do this."

My grandma had tried to stop the party, shaking her head and warning "Bullets don't have no name." Though I argued that no one had ever been shot because the guns were just for show, not for real, my stomach and heart were complaining. On the outside, I played the part of happy "birthday girl." Nobody was going to ruin my party—grandma or gangster.

*Names of gang members throughout the book are fictional street names.

But it happened. After, the party had been going on for three or four hours, Ray Cuz, a Crip leader, started yelling at Bloods and pushing the brothers around. They pushed back, of course. A scuffle between Ray Cuz and Red Dog, who was a Blood, almost got something going. But my mom's boyfriend broke in and asked Ray Cuz to leave. He didn't put up any trouble, but I heard him say to Red Dog, "This ain't over."

*It was a warm fall night, clear with a sky full of stars. I stepped out on the porch to get some air away from the hot, crowded dance floor. Red Dog was standing on the porch stairs looking down the street. I saw a blue and black jeep drive slowly down the middle of the street and stop at the corner. Ray Cuz was driving. Legs was on the passenger side. The jeep parked and Legs crawled out the passenger window. I guess he thought it was cool to leave by the window instead of the door, or maybe the door was broken. Red Dog watched. Dressed in a wool, red and white checked Pendleton shirt, he looked bigger than ever. He really was a **big** brother, stocky and tall too. People called him Red Dog for his light skin and his Blood affiliation.*

When I saw him head out to the corner, I said, "Don't go down there. Let them be." He wasn't paying any attention to me. I knew he'd been drinking. He'd been drinking a lot lately. His mother had died only two months before, and he was trying to drink his sorrow away. I stood on the porch and watched as he walked toward the jeep. He was yelling; they were yelling back, but I couldn't tell what they were saying. Before he reached the corner, I heard firecrackers going off, a whole string of them. Within the sound of the popping firecrackers, I could also hear the sure sharp bang of gun shots. I counted seven shots. I knew Red Dog didn't have a gun on him. The Crips were firing at him.

Red Dog took off running and I lost sight of him. I was sure he was okay because he was running so hard, not like a wounded man. The people inside hadn't heard a thing; they were still dancing and laughing when I went back inside, but I was sick to my stomach. I didn't talk to anyone. I just said, "Party over," and people slowly started to leave.

At 2 a.m. when most of the guests had gone, police officers knocked on my door. They told us Red Dog was dead. He had been dead when his homies delivered him to his father after picking him up in the street. One of the seven bullets had found him, entering under his left arm and coming to a stop in his abdomen. There had been almost no blood. In fact, no one realized he was wounded until they pulled up at Red Dog's house and asked his father to help get him inside. "My boy is dead," his father had quietly said after feeling his son's pulse.

Police questioned my auntie and me, and others who were still there, until 5 a.m. But what could they find out? No one knew anything. Red Dog had been there and then he was not . . . and now he was dead.

Nicky was so angry and sad over Red Dog's death that she vowed to become a Blood, herself. She joined them shortly after this event.

Discussion Questions

1. Nicky hadn't planned on having alcohol at her party. Could she have prevented it? How? Why can alcohol be a problem at a party?

2. Nicky did do some smart things in planning her party. What aspects of the party plan were good ideas? What were possible problems?

3. Red Dog had been drinking to ease the pain of his mother's death. Can you think of other ways to ease emotional pain? What are they?

4. Why do you think Red Dog headed off to meet the Crips? What motives might he have had?

5. Nicky tried to stop Red Dog from going down the street to meet with the Crip members. What else could she have done?

6. Why do you think Nicky didn't tell the others at the party what had happened to Red Dog? Do you think this was a wise choice?

7. How do you think Red Dog's father felt on discovering his son was dead? What do his words and the way they were said tell you about his feelings?

8. Why do you think "no one knew anything" when the police questioned the people at the party, including Nicky and her aunt? Were they telling the truth? If not, why did they pretend not to know?

9. When someone hurts you or people you care about, what is the best response? Nicky decided she would try to hurt those who had hurt her friends. What other options did she have?

10. Nicky joined a gang to seek revenge. What are other reasons young people might join dangerous gangs?

Alcohol and Other Drugs at a Party:

The fun part:

Some people laugh and relax.

Some people dance better.

Some people feel better about

  themselves.

Some people act funny and

  make you laugh.

The not-so-fun part:

Some people get sick and throw up.

Broken lamps, furniture, and people.

Police officers as unexpected guests.

Tempers flare; fights break out

Pregnancy

Ruined friendships

Nicky Talks About Why Kids Join Gangs

A lot of times kids join a gang because they're not getting enough attention at home. Another reason is because they have an older brother or sister or relative they're following. Sometimes, as I did, they do it out of anger, maybe because they lost a close homie or maybe a relative, and they want to get even.

Maybe they might have low self-esteem or none at all. Maybe they just think this is a way to be popular or a way to have an exciting life because they're bored with nothing to do. Older homies may be telling them it's cool instead of the truth, that it's not cool. I would never be a gang member again. It's too dangerous, and I care too much about myself and my family.

Gang members never know if a bullet will strike them when they walk outside. In a gang neighborhood, that's true for everyone, but a gang member has much less of a chance to live than others. To survive, a gang member often has to "slang dope." When I say "slang dope," I mean sell drugs, and you never know when that's going to end because the police are always trying to outsmart you. If they catch you, they throw you in the slammer or jail, and there it goes--something called a felony that will stick with you for the rest of your life. When you go to get an apartment or house, when you go to get a job, they will ask you if you've ever been convicted of a felony. If you lie, you will get caught sooner or later. When you go before the judge, he or she will take your driver's license away. You don't even have to have a license; the judge will take your future license away.

When you're selling drugs, the police are the least of your worries. People who take drugs don't have too many morals. They will shoot you, stab you, run you over to get your dope. A lot of times they don't care who they kill because I know crack smokers who killed their mother. Taking your mother's life over a $20 rock!

To me, a life is worth far more than any amount of money. You can't replace a human life, and I don't care how hard your heart is, you will always have to live with your conscience.

Discussion Questions:

1. How could low self-esteem lead to a young person joining a gang?

2. Older young people who are in gangs sometimes try to get young teens involved in gangs. Why would they do that, knowing how dangerous and destructive gang life is? And why do the younger teens listen to them? Will you listen more to an older teen than to a teacher or a parent? Why or why not?

What is a Gang? - 9

3. Do you think it's fair that a felony stays on your record for life? Why do you think the law requires this record to be preserved? What purpose does it serve?

4. Describe the many dangers of selling drugs. Who gets hurt? Why and how?

5. If someone younger than you asked you about gangs, what would you say? How would you explain the dangers honestly and clearly?

Activities

1. Plan your own 16th birthday party. How would you like to spend it—a party, a family get-together, a small group of friends? How could you insure a safe, fun celebration?
- Make a list of guests.
- Plan the menu of food and drink
- Decide where and when the party will be held.
- Determine safety precautions.

2. Investigate the services available for a depressed teenager like Red Dog or Nicky. Are there counselors at school, church or elsewhere in the community who could help? List possibilities, with names, addresses and phone numbers.

3. Design a "feel good" package that might cheer up someone who is feeling depressed. Include inspirational thoughts; jokes and cartoons; stories about role model examples who overcame hardship; colorful and cheerful pictures; candy, flowers, or other small gifts. Find someone who needs cheering up and take it to him or her. Tell your group how it was received.

4. Invite a counselor who works with teens to speak to the group about depression and how to handle it. Or invite a police officer to talk about safe parties.

5. Cut articles out of magazines and newspapers on gang activity. Share them

with your group and determine what the results of the gang activity were. Were they negative? If so, who was harmed and how? How could the event have been prevented?

6. Create posters that encourage kids to stay out of gangs. Think of ways to appeal to them without scaring them. How could you make positive activity more appealing than joining a dangerous gang? Take your posters to an elementary school. You may be able to set up a time when you could talk to the children and tell them what the posters mean and why you made them.

7. Research the disease of alcoholism. What are its signs and symptoms, and is the tendency to become an alcoholic inherited? What are the effects of alcohol on society in terms of accidents, suicides, crimes, divorce, and domestic violence? Using library and Internet resources, prepare a report. You may want to construct graphs and charts to illustrate what you discover.

Imagine . . .
What if everyone in your group
resolved to help each other
stay out of destructive gangs,
succeed at school,
succeed at home.
You would become a gang with a good purpose.

2
Friends: Love Them or Leave Them

Sometimes it's hard to tell who your friends are. Think about your friends. How can you tell when someone is truly your friend? Ask yourself:

Would a friend . . .
Teach you how to use drugs?
Lend you or sell you a gun?
Tell your secrets?
Tell you a lie?
Take your boyfriend or girlfriend?
Spread bad rumors about you or your family?
Tell you when you're wrong?
Steal from you?
Take but never give?
Make fun of you?
Be afraid of you?
Endanger your life?
Turn his or her back on you?
Die for you?

Nicky Talks About Friendship

You probably think friends come and go, and if you do, that's true. Most friends do come and go, whether they are gang friends or friends you grew up with or went to school with. The friends you never let go of are those you call your brother or sister. That means they are your best friends; no matter what the circumstances, they are your friends. No matter how far away they live from you, they are your friends.

True friends don't let time or distance or colors come between them. They don't let any "he/she said" stuff come between them. Friends are there to help one another out at all times, to listen to problems and give advice. Even if they don't give advice, they listen to your problems and love you no matter what.

But now we're in the 90's, and it's hard to know when to trust someone. Some people act like your friends and then turn against you in a minute, so be careful how you choose your friends. You could lose them in 101 ways. Sometimes so-called friends are setting you up to get shot, shot at, jumped, or beat down. They endanger not only you but also your family. Sometimes so-called friends will steal from you—money, cars, friends, coats, and jewelry, whatever they get their hands on.

It's not good when gang members hang around friends who aren't banging. As my grandma has always said, "Bullets ain't got no name." Bullets don't discriminate; they're color blind and age blind, and will kill or hurt any person who gets in the way. If you have friends who are in dangerous gangs, you might lose them at any time. I don't know how it feels to be pregnant (like a relative of mine), have the baby, and then watch the father get killed. But I do know how it feels to have to bury a homie, which means a very close friend.

My friend was young, intelligent, very fine looking and had a good sense of humor. It was funny for him to be so young but have so much going for him, and I loved him. He was more like my little brother. I always cut or braided his hair. He would come riding with me and my homegirls but after awhile, he moved up, and became a big cat on his own. But now he is dead, and I miss him.

If he had had positive role models, he wouldn't have joined a gang. I sort of introduced him to the streets, but I know people are responsible for the choices they make. Both of us made poor choices, but I was lucky enough to live to make another choice. Rest in peace, Fam Fam.

Discussion Questions

1. What do you think Nicky means by "True friends don't let time or distance or colors come between them. They don't let any "he/she said" stuff come between them"?

2. Why would someone who was supposed to be your friend introduce you to dangerous gang life?

3. What would you do if you discovered a friend had lied to you or stolen from

Friends: Love Them or Leave Them - 13

you? What about a friend who takes your girlfriend or boyfriend?

4. Do you agree with Nicky that "People are responsible for the choices they make"? Explain why you do or do not agree with her. Do you think Nicky should feel responsible for her friend's death?

Who Can Be Trusted?

Nicky admits that she sometimes has trouble knowing whom to trust. People who are trustworthy are known to have what is called "good character." Look over the following list of character traits and check those you think are signs of "good character." Be able to explain why you think so.

Honest	Creative
Intelligent	Respectful of Others
Kind	Understanding
Clever	Positive Attitude about Life
Humorous	Responsible for Own Behavior
Wealthy	Clean
Religious	Good Looking
Dependable	Musical

Are there other qualities besides the ones listed above that you believe a good friend should have?

Nicky's Friend, Sleepy

When Nicky was in the Bloods, she found herself in a leader role sometimes, a big responsibility. The following story tells about an experience she would rather not have had.

We were just cruising down the streets in my car. I was with Lil' Sik, my oldest deuce.* As we turned into the Kwik Mart parking lot I saw my homie Sleepy sitting in his brown Cadillac over in a corner of the lot. He was drinking a 40 oz. bottle of beer. I pulled up next to his car, rolled down my window and asked sharply, "What are you doin'? There's a police car on every corner jus' waiting for someone like you to arrest. Put that bottle down and don't go tryin' to sell anything around here. We jus' saw two police cars down the road."

As we pulled away, I yelled out the window, "And rivals are out. I just had a gun pulled on me up the street, not three blocks away. Stay outa sight."

He responded with his same old unconcerned and easy smile, "I'm all right, boo,* and you be careful." He downed the last in the bottle, looked straight at me, and smiled again. I shook my head and drove away.

We turned up a side street slowly and headed toward the park six or eight blocks away. As we neared the park, I saw three police cars careening around the corner, all headed back where we'd just been, sirens blasting I looked at my deuce and said, "I hope they're not rushin' down there for my homie, Sleepy." Next I hit a u-turn in the middle of the block and headed back to Kwik Mart. My gut told me Sleepy was hit.

When we got back to the Kwik Mart lot, the police were already wrapping the yellow tape around Sleepy's Cadillac. I jumped out of the car and asked the first homie I saw, " Is that Sleepy on the ground?"

The police had placed a sheet over a body lying several feet from Sleepy's car. I could see the bright blood stains soaking through. I knew before I asked. It couldn't be anybody else but Sleepy.

I pushed Lil' Sik back towards the car. I was trying not to act too jumpy or scared around the police because they're always looking for someone acting nervous, someone to lock up in their police car and ask questions. Anyone who looks too nervous is sure to be grabbed. They think anyone showing some feeling must know something. Then they question you—over and over again. I know. In '89, I was forced into a police car and kept for hours after a hit.

I was putting on a good act. In reality, I was feeling bad. There were people running around screaming, throwing up. Some dropped to their knees with others trying to help them stand. My deuce was big-eyed and looked like she was going to cry. This was the closest she'd ever been to a hit. She was only 16.

I could spot rivals in the crowd and I wondered which one was responsible. In my heart I was promising revenge. Alongside my anger was my fear. My deuce and I had just left that scene. Had we stayed only a minute or two longer, we could have been part of it. Maybe one of us would be stretched out on the parking lot with dozens of curious eyes staring at the blood seeping through the sheet, running in small rivers down the pavement.

I'd lost my homie Sleepy, dead at 24. Just a few weeks later I would watch his older brother Boo die in a hospital bed, coughing up blood from the last stages of sickle cell anemia. I'd put my arm around the shoulders of my brother Slim—we'd seen two homies dead in a short space of time.

*deuce: a younger sister, one who looks to an older sister as a role model
*boo: a close friend

Discussion Questions

1. There were police officers throughout the area. What could they have done to stop this crime?

2. Do you agree with the police policy of detaining and questioning those people who show the most emotion?

3. What could Nicky have done to stop this crime?

4. If you were a police officer or detective, how would you go about finding Sleepy's murderer? Why?

5. Nicky is thinking of revenge. Her emotions are mixed—anger and fear. What are her choices?

6. Police officers are often called our "friends," yet some people think of them as "enemies." Why is this the case? How can they be both friends and enemies?

7. Put yourself in Lil Sik's shoes. How do you think she felt about this event? Do you think Nicky is responsible for her? Why or why not?

Handling Peer Pressure

Sometimes friends will try to get you to do something you really don't want to do, something that could cause harm to yourself or others. It's hard to say no to people you view as friends. Here are some tactics to try:

1. Surround yourself with safe people. Try to stay in the midst of a group of people who are not gang related or gang "wannabes."

2. Avoid the people who tend to ask you to join dangerous activities. Don't go places where they might hang out. Go another direction when you see them ahead.

3. Many people think that "Just say No" is a stupid saying because it's easier to suggest it than do it, but, in fact, you can just say "No" when someone wants you to do something you know will cause trouble. Be polite and pleasant, just say, "No, thanks."

4. Move on. Say, "No, thanks," and then quickly walk on.

5. Have a handy excuse such as "No, thanks. I have to get home." Or meet my brother, or go to the store, or whatever sounds reasonable.

6. Use the power of repetition. Every time the person asks, repeat what you just said. Just keep repeating it until the individual gives up asking.

7. Be really honest. Say, "No, that's the kind of thing that could get me in real trouble. I don't want to get my mother or the police on my case. Sorry."

8. Offer an alternative. Say, "I'd rather go over to the gym and shoot some hoops. Want to join me?" or "Let's do something a little less dangerous. Want to come over to my house and listen to my new CD?" Sometimes they are just waiting for someone to talk them out of getting in trouble by suggesting something else.

9. Act like you think they're kidding. Say, "What? You're kidding, right? Man, if we did that, we'd be in deep trouble. No, thank you kindly."

Friends: Love Them or Leave Them - 17

10. Whatever tactic you try, keep in mind the issue of respect. If you treat them with respect by responding in a polite, friendly manner, their response will usually be positive. Have the attitude that you respect their decisions, but you make your own.

Activities

1. Research sickle cell anemia. What are its symptoms? How is it treated? Whom does it afflict? Can it be cured? Is there anything we can do to help friends keep from getting this disease? What diseases are teens particularly at risk of getting, and how can they be prevented?

2. Making friends is sometimes considered difficult, but sometimes losing bad friends is even more difficult. Brainstorm with another person or a group ways to make friends, then brainstorm ways to get rid of bad friends who have shown themselves to be untrustworthy and uncaring. Make a list of ideas for each, and share them with another individual or group.

3. Interview a police officer or detective. Ask him or her what the prescribed procedures after a murder is committed are. How does he or she decide who or where to ask questions? Write a report on your findings.

4. Interview an adult about his or her best friend. Ask what qualities this person has that qualify him or her to be a best friend? Take notes and report to your group.

5. Many people will tell you their best friend is a pet, such as a dog or a cat. What qualities do animals have that could make them best friends? What qualities do they lack? Discuss this idea with another person or group.

6. Nicky has a choice to make. Plot her decision by making a list of alternatives she has, providing the pros and cons of each. Do the same for Lil' Sik. Use the format given on the next page.

18 - *Ask Nicky*

Problem: What to do about Sleepy's murder.		
Nicky Alternatives:	Pros	Cons
1.		
2.		
3.		
4.		
Lil' Sik Alternatives:	Pros	Cons
1.		
2.		
3.		
4.		

Imagine . . . what if each of you decided to be a true friend to each person in this group? Trust and caring would develop in the group, and each person would experience friendship and good feeling.

3
The Meaning of Family

A family in the 90's is defined as "the people an individual lives with, not necessarily blood-related." Families in the 90s come in all kinds. No longer composed of only Mom, Dad, and children, they now take many other forms. Think of the many kinds of families you have noticed. Who is a part of your family right now? Has your family changed over the years?

Families are something like gangs. They can be a group of people with a common purpose. They can do good or cause harm. In a family, their common purpose could be to help each other succeed and be happy, and in many families this is exactly what family members strive to do. Unfortunately, families are like any other group. Sometimes things go wrong. People get sick, angry, confused, or hurt, and then the rest of the group must suffer with them because people who live together have a definite effect on each other.

When Nicky was a small girl, her family had problems. This is her true story. . .

Nicky's Mom's Story

When I was in the third or fourth grade, my family had some serious problems. We were driving in our car, my mom at the wheel and a woman cousin sitting next to her. My little brother Slim, my cousin Ty-Ty, and I were in the back seat. My mom's boyfriend knew my mom was trying to break up with him, and he wanted her to speak with him just one more time. He ran out to the car and begged her to roll the window down so he could talk to her. He said, "Just roll the window down a little bit, baby, and talk to me." As soon as she did, he started giving her his sweet talk. "Baby, I don't want you to leave me. Our relationship can change for the better if we let it."

My mom was leaving him because he had been physically violent to her, and she didn't want us kids to be around that kind of thing. He would act nice around our male relatives, but he would show his mean personality when it was just my mom and us. My mom said, "My kids are so important to me. I can't take it anymore, and they can't take it anymore."

"Baby, get out of the car so I can talk to you without your family being around," he kept sweet-talking to her.

I was yelling, "Don't get out of the car, Momma. Please don't get out of the car!" We were terrified because we knew how he could be. Not too many kids will speak up when the mother and boyfriend are feuding because if he doesn't care about the mother, he surely doesn't care about the kids.

My mom stepped out of the car because he was trying to open the door. He was using both of his hands, so she didn't know he had a butcher knife in his pants waist hidden from view. He kept saying, "We can work this out, baby." He wanted her to go with him, but when she refused he pulled out that butcher knife and started stabbing her. He stabbed her three or four times and then ran away with the knife. My mother passed out at the side of the car. Her cousin got her in the car somehow, and we took her to the hospital. I was the oldest child, but all I could do was hold onto my little brother Slim, who was crying in my arms.

My mom didn't press charges. She called it love, but she didn't go back to him. Now I'm grown up, and I know no man better ever put his hands on me like that man did to my mom.

The Meaning of Family - 21

Discussion Questions

1. Why do you think a man would take a butcher knife to a woman he loved and wanted to stay with him?

2. What alternatives did the man have? What could he have done to get his girlfriend and family back?

3. Did Nicky do the right thing by telling her mother what to do? What would you have done?

4. What reasons can you give for Nicky's mother not pressing charges? Do you think she did the right thing?

5. What do you think Nicky and her brother may have learned from this event? Will this experience make them stronger in the future?

Parents aren't Perfect

Sometimes parents have problems. It's hard to hold down a job, raise a family, pay the bills, and care for children. Sometimes parents make mistakes— like using alcohol and other drugs to relieve pain, like fighting with each other and being abusive to each other and other members of the family. Children in a family having problems don't have many options, but they can find ways to cope without bringing more problems on the family or on themselves.

If a child or teen has problems at home, what are possible solutions? Look at the following list, and check the ones you think would bring the best results:

1. Find a best friend you can trust and tell him or her your problems.

2. Find another relative not living in your home that you can talk to or go to when times are hard.

3. Get involved in sports. This will take up some of the energy anger can cause and improve your health.

4. Run away from home.

5. Talk to your school counselor.

6. Talk to the minister of your church.

7. Get involved in community activities: YWCA, YMCA, Boys and Girls Club, church youth groups.

8. Escape through reading or movies.

9. Find an adult you can talk to.

10. Take drugs and drink alcohol to feel better.

11. Hurt someone, so someone else will hurt as much or more than you do.

Can you think of other ideas? Nicky chose one of the options above. She was lucky to have a grandmother who was always there for her. The following is a letter Nicky wrote to her grandmother, whom she always called Ma.

Nicky's Letter to her Grandma

Nicky and her grandmother, "Ma"

June, 1998

Dear Ma,
I think about all the good times we have had together from the time when I was little until now, but it doesn't stop. The love just grows regardless of what you know about me. I can never repay you for all the things you have done to help me. But there is nothing I wouldn't do for you, my favorite grandma, always known to me as Ma. No matter what the situation, no one or nothing can come between us.

When I was little and my mom's boyfriend would beat her up, I would call my ol' faithful Ma and Pa to come and get me because I couldn't take so much physical and emotional violence. To me, Ma, you have always left love in your footprints. Every time I think about you, I picture you sitting in your recliner chair with a smile, wiggling your toes, and eating a Twinky or chocolate cupcake, making me feel special to be by your side eating with you. I think of us watching our favorite shows and eating our favorite treats.

You encouraged me so much. To me, you saw my steps before I even walked them, and you gave me the most support. Every time I was sick you always had more than a lot of grandma love for me. You gave me courage to face my problems, and if you hadn't pressed the issue for me to believe in my dreams, I wouldn't be the person I am today. You told me how pretty I was, and how beautiful my smile was. My self-esteem wouldn't be as high as it is without you.

All the times when I was bad, you still stood by my side. I remember when the rivals came and broke your big ol' picture window. You didn't put me out of your house as everyone was telling you. There wasn't any yelling. I told you how it happened, and you understood and kept on supporting me. You were by me 100 percent, and when you caught me running away at the age of 18 when I could have just walked away but I knew how it was going to hurt the both of us, you understood. I'm sorry for worrying you all the times I did, and I'm very happy you're here to see my positive improvement.

I'm thankful for having such a sweet, caring, and very understanding grandma. Whenever I felt like coming to your house you never told me no. The doors have always been open, and I know they will remain open.

I've got a lot of friends who call you grandma and respect you for who you are and what you and I believe. You always told me to respect my elders, and you said to respect those who respect you.

You taught me that old saying "Do unto others how you would want to be done to you." And it's a true saying. If a person lives by it, he or she would live longer. You also taught me about God up above who will never leave me nor forsake me. That's true, too, and without God and you, Ma, I would be nothing today. I might not even be here today. God bless you, Ma.

Love,

Your granddaughter, Nicole

Discussion Questions:

1. What are the characteristics of Nicky's grandmother? What kind of person is she? Give as many descriptive words as you can.

2. What kind of influence has she had on Nicky? What has she taught her?

3. If a teenage child does something wrong, do you think the parent or grandparent should make them leave the home? If a son or daughter is involved in gangs, should he or she be asked to leave the home? Why or why not?

4. Do you think the saying (which is paraphrased from the Bible) "Do unto others how you would want to be done to you" is wise? Could following this help you to live longer? How? How do you think it helped Nicky?

Family Squabbles

Every family has squabbles (arguments, disagreements). That's just what happens when people live together, but there are ways to resolve these kinds of conflicts; some ways work better than others. When an argument occurs people usually do one of the following:

1. Disappear
This means they either leave the room or the house, or they get very quiet and don't respond anymore. They have either removed themselves physically or mentally.

2. Fight
This means they try to win by hurting the other person either physically or emotionally. They might use their fists or a weapon, or they might use their tongues by saying the meanest things they can think of to hurt the other person's feelings.

3. Give in
In order to avoid argument or discussion, sometimes people just give in and say, "OK, whatever." They let the other person have his or her way just to

keep from disagreeing.

4. Convince

They might try very hard, and they might succeed in getting the other person to see things their way. This is fair unless they use bribery, guilt, or threat to get agreement.

5. Negotiate

In this case, both sides of the argument have the opportunity to say exactly what they think—as long as they don't call the other person names, lie, or exaggerate. All sides of the problem are discussed honestly and openly, each side talking without interruption. Then alternatives can be discussed and the best one agreed to.

Which of the above methods do you usually use? Only one of them allows both sides to win. Which one? Every situation is different, and sometimes it is necessary to allow only one side to win, but negotiation, when possible, can satisfy both sides.

Role-play a Negotiation

Think of a conflict that happened at school or at home. Ask two people to play the roles of the two parties. Have them follow the steps below to resolve the conflict:

1. Each side explains how he or she sees the problem without interruption from the other side. In their explanations, they may not criticize the other person or call him or her names. They must tell about the problem truthfully and without dramatization (adding words, gestures, or facial expressions that make it seem worse).

2. Both sides brainstorm possible resolutions. Brainstorm means to think up solutions quickly without judging them at the time. The possibilities are written down on paper or on a writing board.

3. Both sides go over the possible resolutions, discussing fully what they mean.

4. Both sides agree on a resolution, which may require adding or subtracting something from those given in order to achieve agreement.

5. Both sides should monitor the agreement to make sure it happens as agreed. If not, they need to re-negotiate.

6. If they cannot come up with an agreed-upon resolution, they might have to call in a third party, one who can be objective and not take sides, to determine the best resolution.

Discuss the role-play. Did both sides appear to be happy with the resolution? Think about the other methods of handling conflict. Are there situations when something other than negotiation would be the best method to apply? Give examples.

Nicky, her brother Slim, and her mother Nola

Nicky's Mom has Become her Best Friend

My mom is my best friend. She knows when something is wrong, and there's barely anything she wouldn't do for me. Yes, we've had our ups and downs just like other best friends and mothers and daughters. No matter how much we get into it, we always respect each other.

In 1996, my homies gave my mom and me the mother and daughter award and have been giving us that award ever since. They love to see Nick and Nola coming because they know we're coming with laughter and fun. If more parents would spend time with their kids, I think there would be less violence.

My friends love and respect my mom, always have, even though she loves and respects both sides, Bloods and Crips. At first, it was hard for me to understand this, but now that I'm older I see she is right. My mom is known for throwing neighborhood barbeque parties--for both sides, for everyone in the neighborhood. She buys all the food, and I do all the work. She knows that kids need something to do that is fun, not dangerous or illegal. My friends call her Mama Woodlawn--that's the name of our neighborhood.

My mom, my best friend, is not ashamed to say that she used to use alcohol and crack cocaine, but she has been clean for almost ten years. In the last five years, we have become very close. She has been there for me, a good example, a strong support. I know I wouldn't be where I am without her support.

Discussion Questions

1. Why do you think grandparents, rather than parents, are often the ones children go to when they are troubled?

2. Why do you think it has only been the last five years that Nicky and her mom have become close?

3. Do you think barbeques with both Crips and Bloods attending is a good idea or a dangerous idea? Explain your answer.

4. Why do you think Nicky's mom is not ashamed for people to know she used to use alcohol and crack cocaine? Do you know people who have "kicked" a drug or alcohol habit? How have their lives changed? We can see some of the ways Nicky's mom's life has changed? What are they?

Activities

1. Write a letter to a parent, grandparent, or another person who has helped you in some way. Tell them how they helped you and thank them for being there when you needed them. Mail or deliver the letter.

2. Plan an activity you and your family could do together. It doesn't have to cost much money or even require you to leave home. It might be watching a special video together with popcorn or other treats. It might be celebrating a special event such as a birthday or holiday. If it's winter, try having an

indoor picnic with a blanket on the floor to sit on and a picnic lunch to eat. Ask a parent or brother or sister to help you get ready for this event.

3. In a private journal or on paper kept in a secret place, write out a plan to follow if you find yourself in a dangerous position in your family. It might include phone numbers of people who can help, and information on youth shelters, counselors, and ministers.

4. Practice using the conflict resolution steps in a family quarrel. Report to the group how it worked or didn't work.

5. Make a teaching video of conflict resolution using negotiation. Show it to other groups, explaining the steps and setting up role-play situations for them.

6. Put together a photo album of your family, labeling each picture. Write stories to go with some of the pictures.

Imagine . . .
What if every conflict were resolved through negotiation? Consider conflicts between countries, groups, and individuals.
How would our world change?

4
Another View of School

Teens like to grumble about school; they've been doing it for ages, just like older people like to grumble about their jobs. But in both cases—school and work—how you look at them can make a big difference in what you get out of them. Many people think that the effort you put into school or work is the most important thing. That's important, but not nearly as important as how you look at them, what you see them as.

School is many things, not just a place where teachers try to help you learn knowledge and skills. Examine the list below and check those items that you believe can be found at school:

Books	Hate	Excitement
Computers	Administrators	Music
Teachers	Friends	Jobs
Fun	Enemies	Conversation
Food	Fear	Pain
Counselors	Fights	Sports
Boredom	Groups	Love

Did you check almost all of the items? Can you think of a single place on earth that could offer you more? Not all of the items are pleasant, but all of them teach you something. You could watch television every day for a year and not come close to experiencing all of these things. School is a valuable resource overflowing with opportunities to learn.

Nicky did not finish school. She quit when she needed only three more credits to graduate. Why would she quit when she was so close to finishing? Here is her story . . .

I was a great student when I was younger, but when I got to high school, my mind wouldn't let me do the things I wanted to do. I guess my mind is somewhat stronger than my body. I wanted to go to class, but my mind wouldn't let me, so I remained in the hallways, or if I went to class I was just a class clown, didn't take it seriously. I wanted to make others laugh probably because I was hurting inside. I never really sat and thought about my behavior.

In spite of all this, the teachers loved me. Half the time I think they passed me just because they liked me because I really didn't learn a darn thing. But I only blame myself, no one else. I was very active in my gang at that time, and it affected my mind and my behavior.

It was the gang problem that finally pushed me out of school. The high school passed a new policy that wouldn't allow dressing in gang colors—red, black, green, burgundy. I couldn't wear anything that looked related to gangs. Everything I owned was either red or black, my gang colors. I didn't have anything else, and I didn't have enough money to go buy new clothes. To buy new clothes, I would have had to get out on the streets and sell dope, risking my life again. I also had trouble giving up my gang identity. That was who I was.

So I dropped out. I just said, "Forget it," and I walked down the hallway saying good bye but telling my real friends to stay in school. "Gang banging is not worth giving up school," I warned. Sure enough, the 10 or 15 people I hung around with did stay in school, and they did graduate. I think this is great and I love them for that. I think they used me as an example of the wrong thing to do. They saw me out on the street, always getting guns pulled on me, never backing down, willing to get myself killed if I had to. They knew I'd been shot a couple of times, and they realized bullets aren't just for males; females get shot too. They thought, "If it happened to Nicky, it can happen to any one of us."

At the time, all I could think of was, "I'm bad. I can't be beat. I can't be killed."

I'm not a punk anymore. Now I wish I had stayed in school and spent my last dollar on new clothes. But I was trying to be hard, even though I didn't want to. The streets had taken me under.

Nicky in front of Grant High School, Portland, Oregon

Oh, I really regret not staying in school. I didn't listen to my elders. It was like what people say now, "Talk to the hand 'cause my mind doesn't understand." So I did what I chose to do— fall on my rear alone, crawl, and then walk, and that's what I did.

What I am saying is coming straight from my heart. If you're thinking about joining a gang, don't do it. If you're thinking about quitting school, don't do it. No one can tell me I don't know what I'm talking about because I have lived that life. Remember, if the school is doing its job, they'll see you headed the wrong way, and if they don't, don't be scared to ask them to steer you. Don't act like you've got too much pride, or you're scared, or embarrassed. Get as much help as you can.

Discussion Questions

1. Why do you think some kids choose to be class clowns, to hang out in the halls instead of going to class? Nicky said she was hurting inside. What

could be some other reasons?

2. Do you think teachers sometimes grade on how much they like you? Or don't like you? What makes you think so? How should students be graded— on how well behaved they are, how well they pass tests, or other ways?

3. Do you think schools should restrict what students wear to school? What do you think about wearing uniforms to school? Is this a good idea? Why or why not?

4. Nicky says, "That was who I was." What does she mean? Can people change their perceptions of "who they are"? How?

5. Does it seem strange to you that Nicky would advise her friends to stay in school even though she, herself, was leaving? How can you explain this?

6. Nicky was serving as a kind of reverse role model for her friends. Explain how her bad behavior produced good behavior in her friends. Can you think of other examples of this in life?

7. Nicky is sincere and emotional when she tells you to stay in school and stay out of gangs. How is she different from the adults who tell you the same thing?

Teachers are People, Too

Teachers, like parents and all other people, can make mistakes. Sometimes what they do and say right now may seem like a mistake, and then later you may realize that they knew what they were talking about. Other times, because they're angry, unaware, or just plain tired, they might make a mistake, perhaps one that affects you personally. Think about a teacher you really liked. What was it about this person that you liked? How did he or she make you feel?

Nicky remembers a favorite teacher . . .

I don't think I ever told Ms. Jackson how much I appreciated her until recently. I remember, but maybe she doesn't, that she stood by me when rivals tried to get me at school. She was right by my side protecting me--without a bulletproof vest! I remember her walking from the front door of the school to my auntie's car to tell me, "Bye and stay safe. I mean it, Nick."

My own mom was barely clean from crack, so it was really hard for me to trust her as far as talking on a mother/daughter level, but I was able to trust Ms. Jackson.

Even though I was class clown and tried to get out of her Social Studies class for an easier one, she wouldn't let me. She came to me and offered me an 8th period class just for extra credit to see me walk across the stage in 1990, graduating on time. She helped me because I know she believed in me.

When my homies were after me to skip my 8th period class, they would say, "Nick, there goes Ms. Jackson," and they would hide me. From the bottom of my heart I would hurt inside because that class was helping me, but I was caught up in peer pressure and thought having fun was more important than my education. That was a big fake fairytale.

When Red Dog was killed, Ms. Jackson asked the school to provide counseling for those who were involved. We wanted and needed to talk so bad. All she could do was send us to the nurse's office, which just drove me crazier because all they did was ask how we felt. They had no real answers for us, but she tried and we tried, and she didn't give up.

Ms. Jackson used to have fashion shows for the high school kids. I believe it was the last one she did where my homies and I on a dare jumped up on stage to show off our fresh Nike suits. We even bowed on time with the rest of the models. The next day I was called to the Dean's office and I was suspended for a week. I remember they wouldn't let me go to the prom with Keith T. who was the finest young man in the senior class. He picked me up anyway in a rental car, but I gave him permission to take another girl while I watched through the windows at the Schnitzer Hall.

Ms. Jackson helped me get back in school by telling the Dean I only had three credits left to earn for graduation. She wanted to see me graduate so I could get away from the Portland streets. I let her down. I quit school, but I want her to know that I have much love for her, and, in case the community doesn't know, they need more teachers like Ms. Jackson.

Now I'm staying here to give back to the community. I believe that if kids have someone to talk to who has been on the streets, life for them won't go as bad as mine did. I've been shot twice, and people tell me my life has been spared for a reason. I believe helping others, as Ms. Jackson did, is the reason.

Discussion Questions

1. What kinds of things did Ms. Jackson do that may be different from the things most teachers do?

2. Though Nicky really liked Ms. Jackson, why do you think she was unable to stay in school as her teacher wanted her to do?

3. What behavior got Nicky in trouble at school? Would your school allow this kind of behavior? Why or why not?

4. Is there any reason to believe that some of Ms. Jackson's help actually made a difference in Nicky's attitude? Explain.

What is Education Anyway?

Many people think of education as a seeing tool. It spreads light on your world. The amount of education you have determines how well you can see in this world. The more you learn, the better you can see. Some people view the world by the light of a single match; others carry huge, searching spotlights. The more you can see, the more you know and understand.

Other people see education as freedom. Think of the person who cannot read or write. How free is he or she? Imagine all one would miss if unable to read the many messages we are confronted with each day. Think of the multitude of occupations that are closed to those who cannot read or write.

Why do you think the government requires young people to attend school? Many other countries have no such requirement. Are you getting enough out of your time spent in school? How could things improve? Are there enough classrooms, teachers, books and other materials? Most important of all, do the students have a good attitude about learning? Do most of them try, and are most of them succeeding. Discuss this in your group.

Make a list of ways your school could improve. You may want to use this later in completing one of the unit's activities.

Be in Charge of Your Own Education

Learning happens everywhere all the time, not only in schools, not only at the hands of teachers. You can guide your own education. It should be firmly attached to your goals. Figure out what you want to be doing in the future, and then figure out what knowledge and skills you must have to do this.

Select your courses at school to correspond with your goals. For example, if you want to go into a science profession, you will need to take as many courses in science and math as your high school offers. If you're interested in business, take accounting and computer courses. Whatever you want to do, even if it's being a brick layer or carpenter, something you could learn on the job, a high school diploma is important. Many apprenticeship programs in these skill areas won't take people who haven't graduated from high school.

If a college education is necessary to fulfill your goals, start looking into financing right away. Your school counselor can tell you how to finance a college education, but getting a part-time job and saving what you can is a good start.

Meanwhile, take advantage of every opportunity to learn what you need and want to learn. People who are engaged in the kind of work you want to do can advise you and provide valuable knowledge and skills. Libraries and Internet sources are other ways to learn. Magazines, films, clubs and groups, businesses, newspapers, conferences--so many sources of information await you.

Studies show that people learn best when they have chosen what they want to study and when they can see how that information will help them meet their personal goals. Sometimes it may seem as though you are jumping through hoops, other people's hoops. But if that jump is one step on your way to where you want to be, you'll find later on that it was worth your effort.

The best thing about education is that once you have it, nobody can take it away from you. Once knowledge is in your head, no one can steal it, repossesses it, or even borrow it without your personal permission.

Activities:

1. Do an inventory of your school. What services are available to you? Make an annotated list of everything available through your school. Consider meal programs, classes offered, school clubs and organizations, sports, counselors, special programs such as tutoring, mentoring, business apprenticeships. Remember that it is your school, set up to guide you and teach you. Take advantage of the programs that can help.

2. Think of all the things you'd like to learn about. Write them down and after each one, list the different ways you could learn about that subject or acquire that skill. You may think of books in the library, textbooks, teachers, magazines, videos, people, observation. There are many ways to learn what you want, and you can guide your own learning.

3. Alone or in a group, choose one of the following statements and use every souce of information you can find to come to your own opinion of the issue. Your research might include interviewing people, looking things up in the library, or surfing the Web. Report your findings and conclusions to the larger group.

   - Teenagers should be treated as adults when they commit serious crimes.

   - Uniforms should be required in public schools.

   - Exploring the Internet is a dangerous activity for teens.

   - Computers are better than teachers.

   - Attendance at school should not be required after the age of 14.

4. Test the services in your school. Make an appointment with a counselor to discuss your future, perhaps college scholarships or special programs; mentor or tutor programs to help you succeed. See how easy or difficult it is to see a counselor. Attend meetings of some of the clubs or organizations in which you may have an interest. How easy is it to join? Were you welcomed and encouraged to join? Make an appointment with the school nurse or school clinic to discuss a health question. Was it easy or difficult to get an appointment? Was it helpful? Report to the larger group on your discoveries.

5. Do a survey of the community colleges in your area. What are the entrance requirements, fees, etc? What kind of financial aid do they offer? In what fields do they specialize? Report to the group.

6. Investigate what the school or public library has on study skills, methods to become a better student. Skim the material, take notes on what you feel is important, and report to the group.

7. Develop a plan to improve your attendance and grades at school. Brainstorm ideas with a friend, parent, or other trusted person. Write down those ideas that you think will work for you and put them into practice. Reward yourself with something fun or relaxing (for example, watching a favorite TV show, eating a special snack, or shooting baskets with a friend) every day you follow your plan.

8. Organize a "Study Pals" group that meets each week or twice a week to do homework together, helping each other, keeping each other on track. Find a convenient place to meet and invite two or three friends who might be interested.

9. Using the list your group made of ways your school could improve, write a letter to the principal of your school outlining your views. Be careful not to write as though you are blaming him or her. Be sure all of the items are ones that can be changed. Afterwards invite him or her to come to your class to discuss the list.

Imagine . . .
What if everyone had the opportunity to learn as
much as possible?
How would our world change?

5
Looking for a Role Model

A role model is a person you look up to and admire, someone on whom you'd like to model your own life. Positive role models inspire us to have dreams and to work hard to make them come true. Just as it is easier to learn a new skill if you have someone who does it well to watch and copy, it is easier to have a good life if you have someone's good example to follow

Sometimes people think that role models have to be movie stars, athletes, or other kinds of celebrities. It's easy to see that Michael Jordan is a superb basketball player, that Jennifer Lopez is a beautiful and talented actress, and Jesse Jackson and Robert Dole are respected political leaders. However, we see them from a distance. We only see them at their best. Do you ever wonder what they are like when the spotlight is not on them?

Maybe you don't have to look in the newspapers or on television to find role models. Look around you at the people you have in your life right now: parents and grandparents, brothers, sisters, neighbors, teachers, friends. You have the opportunity to see these people in ordinary circumstances. Do you have a teacher who always treats his or her students with respect no matter who they are or what they do? Maybe you have one who is always cheerful—even when things go wrong. Do you have a mother or a father who gets up early every morning and goes to work no matter how tired she or he may be? Do you have a big sister or brother who helps you with your homework or shows you how to cook, use a computer or play basketball? Do you have a neighbor who brings a meal over when your mother is sick? Maybe a friend of your family has given up using drugs and is now attending college.

If you pay attention, you'll see that you have many positive people around you who are doing their jobs, helping other people, leading their lives in a way that makes the world a better place to be. Watch how they live their lives; they can be a great help to you in reaching your goals just by being there for you to watch. Sometimes they will even go out of their way to help you.

Nicky's Positive Role Model

Nicky has always thought of her Aunt Jovita as her role model:

My Auntie Jovita, whom I called JoJeya and still do to this very day, is a person I respect a lot, someone I want to be like, and I am like her in many ways.

We both love Chinese food, but our favorite home cooked meal is tacos. We probably would be able to eat them all day every day if we only had to cook for ourselves. But I am like her in more important ways. My auntie is the kind of person you can call any time to talk to for any reason, and you can count on her to hold any secret. I am like that, too. I learned it from her.

Aunt Jovita, Nicky's Grandma, and Nicky

Once when I was 10 or 11 my little brother Slim, who was maybe 6 or 7, wanted to buy a watergun, but he didn't have enough money. So I switched the price tag, not knowing I was on camera. All I remember is I gave my brother exactly $3.99, just enough to buy the watergun. Then I left and he was to meet me with Auntie JoJeya in another store. I remember he was just barely tall enough to reach the counter.

The store people followed him right to the other store where I was waiting with my auntie. I kept on denying I had switched the price tag till they told me to "either tell the truth or your brother is going to jail."

I looked at my auntie, then looked at my brother Slim, and he was crying. "Okay," Jojeya said, "tell them and I won't tell your grandma or pa."

I said I did it. To this day my auntie has never told my grandma or anyone, even though I'm 26 now and it really doesn't matter. Ever since then I haven't stolen so much as a five-cent piece of bubblegum.

I also get funny feelings when things are about to go wrong like my Auntie Jojeya does. I had a funny feeling the night of my sixteenth birthday party when Red Dog was killed. Auntie Jojeya used to get funny feelings about me. Sometimes she'd come to pick me up long before school was out because she had a funny feeling. Back then rivals were always coming after me with car jacks, bats, poles, anything that would knock me unconscious. I didn't want to take a gun to school. I knew in my mind and heart that it wasn't worth carrying a gun to school because nine out of ten times you will reach for that gun and use it. I just trusted my auntie to pick my homies and me up. She did it because she loved us. Even if she didn't agree with anything we were doing, she tried her hardest to understand.

Ten Reasons why Auntie Jojeya is my role model. . .

> *1. She's beautiful.*
> *2. She's proud.*
> *3. She's a Christian.*
> *4. She has a strong heart.*
> *5. She loves to work.*
> *6. She is caring.*
> *7. She is responsible.*
> *8. She never gave up on me.*
> *9. She has a good marriage*
> *10. She is a good mother to her two children.*

Discussion Questions

1. Nicky learned something from the experience of getting caught switching price tags. What do you think her little brother Slim might have learned? Who was his role model?

2. If you were Nicky's Auntie Jojeya, would you have done what she did? Would you have told Nicky's parents? Would you have picked up Nicky and her

homies at school? Why or why not?

3. Nicky was smart enough not to carry a gun to school. What are the pros and cons of carrying guns anywhere?

Who's a Positive Role Model?

Do positive role models have lots of money, promising careers, big houses, and nice cars? Sometimes, but not always. They do share some qualities in common, however. Successful people, whether their success is raising a healthy child, winning the Most Valuable Player award in a sport, or running their own business, almost always have all or many of the following characteristics:

Positive Role Models Make the Most of Themselves.
They find out what their skills and talents are, and they work hard to make them better. For example, if they have a talent in art, they might take art classes, spend lots of time working on learning and perfecting art techniques, study the work of famous artists, and invest in good art supplies. Everyone has talent. Sometimes a person may have talents he or she hadn't thought of as talents, for example, the ability to handle small children, cheer up someone who's sad, organize and make messy places neat, fix a tasty meal, listen carefully, work with very small parts, fix broken toys, run very fast, or sing, dance, and tell jokes. Positive role models take the things they can do well and perfect them.

Positive Role Models Take Good Care of Themselves.
It is not selfish to be good to yourself. In fact, the nicest thing you can do for those who love you is to take care of yourself. Then they won't have to worry about you. Furthermore, if you are taking good care of yourself, you are able to help others more. Think what it means to take care of yourself. Getting enough to eat and enough sleep are only part of the task. Positive role models keep themselves away from dangerous drugs that can hurt the body and mind. They stay in safe places with safe people. They are kind to themselves, remind themselves of their good qualities and all the other good things in the world, and keep their minds at peace.

Positive Role Models Have Goals.
They think what they would like their futures to hold and set goals to achieve those things. They ask themselves, "Do I want a college education, a good job, a nice home and car, a family? Do I want to live or visit some special place? Do I want to learn a certain skill?" They make a list of the things they want in their lives and

consult it often to be sure they're headed in the right direction.

Positive Role Models Have Vision.

To have vision is to be able to see. In this case, vision means the ability to see yourself in your mind actually accomplishing your goals. Positive role models imagine themselves in the jobs they've always wanted, imagine themselves driving the cars they want, living in the houses they want—whatever they want to be doing in the future, they make sure to paint a vivid picture in their minds of themselves actually doing or being their dreams. They know that if you can't imagine yourself ever accomplishing those things, you won't be able to achieve them. You must believe in yourself and believe in your dreams.

Nicky, her high school friend, Cool Nutz and Angie B. Cool Nutz is now a well known rapper having produced several popular CD's of his own raps.

Positive Role Models Turn Negatives into Positives.

Bad things happen all the time, even to the best of people. Successful people know this because bad things happen to them. A business fails, an accident occurs, sickness arrives—all kinds of bad things happen all the time. Positive role models pick themselves up, shake off the trouble, and try again. They don't let things keep them down. They find whatever positive they can in whatever has changed in their lives, adjust their goals, and continue on their way.

Positive Role Models Love and Appreciate Life.

This is the most important quality of all because if a person loves life, this special life he or she has been given, he or she will take care of it, value it, and do good things with it. A positive role model knows that not only his or her own life is valuable and precious but also the lives of other people and other living things. Everything and everyone is here for a purpose. Positive role models figure out their purpose and fit happily into life with every other living thing.

Look around you. Can you spot some positive role models? By all means, they aren't perfect people, but they're doing the best they can, working on their dreams, and loving and appreciating life each day.

Some Famous Positive Role Models

Magic Johnson, professional basketball player for the L.A. Lakers. Magic was diagnosed HIV positive a number of years ago. Did he hang his head, go hide in a cave, and wait to become sick with AIDS? No, he worked hard to be an excellent father and husband, continued to perfect his basketball game, helped others wherever and however he could. He is still alive today, still trying to do his best.

Representative Margaret Carter started out as a single mom in Portland, Oregon. She worked her way through school, became a college teacher and then was elected a representative in the Oregon State Legislature. She has helped bring many good things in the way of human services and economic development to her African American community. She has nine grown children.

Tara Lipinski, 1998 Gold Medalist in Woman's Figure Skating. Tara, though only 16, has worked hard most of her life to perfect her skating performance. When she won the Gold Medal in the 1998 Olympic Games and became the youngest individual in history to win a gold medal in the Winter Games she said that she had always felt she was going to do this, and now she had done it.

Negative Role Models

Negative role models have some or all of the opposites of the characteristics given for positive role models. They can cause pain not only for the people around them but for themselves. Sometimes their only problem is that they have never been able to recognize the positive role models around them or, worse, perhaps they have never had positive role models.

Think what the opposite of each of the positive characteristics might be. Do you know people who have these opposite characteristics? They may be close friends or family, but try to avoid them if possible because they can drag you down. Sometimes standing up to them can help them realize they're headed the wrong direction; sometimes it can be dangerous. Think carefully before responding to negative role models. Ignoring them may be the best way to handle them.

You are a Role Model

You are constantly watched by children younger than you are, brothers and sisters, cousins, friends and neighbors. Children learn by watching and copying others. How can you be sure your behavior serves as a positive example?

Nicky knows about this:

Some people can be role models in a negative way and think it's the thing to be. I know I did, and I was just as negative as all outdoors.

I had a deuce (a young person who looked up to me), who acted so much like me in so many different ways. She was or should I say still is loud, wild, and doesn't care whether she lives or dies. She is what we call a "bad moma jamma," which means she's BAD. She will fight no matter who it is. She doesn't care if she wins or loses, although I've never seen her lose. She used to look at me and say, "Nick, should I get with her or just leave her alone?" It used to depend on how much I liked or disliked the person she was getting ready to fight.

She and another girl I called my "baby deuce" because she was so much younger used to fight, shoot, spray mace, stab, and drive crazy in the street. I was their negative role model; they looked up to me.

Now I'm hoping I can turn some of this around by being a positive role model. I have younger relatives, but I would never ever tell them to throw up any gang signs or even let them know anything at all about the gang life, but if they ask questions, I'm all ears. And I will tell them the truth.

Discussion Questions

1. What can Nicky do now to help the deuces she trained to be gangsters? Is it too late to help them?

2. Why do you think kids often follow the example of older kids rather than their parents or other adults?

3. Children, and older people, too, sometimes model their behavior and words on television shows. You see little kids playing television characters all the time. Is this healthy?

Activities

1. Think of five people whom you consider a positive role model for you. Write their names down and under each name write the reasons this person is a positive role model for you. What characteristics of this person would you like to develop? Talk about one or two of these people with your group members.

2. Write a letter to a famous person you consider a positive role model. Tell him or her you appreciate his or her positive example. You might want to share some of your own goals in your letter.

3. Look through a newspaper. You will find many examples of positive and negative role models. Cut out several of each type and tell your group members about them explaining how and why you think they are positive or negative role models.

4. Think about the characters in television shows. Do some of them seem to be positive role models? Why? Share your ideas with your group members.

5. With your group, brainstorm your own list of positive qualities you think a role model should display. Create a poster with the final list upon which the group has agreed.

Imagine. . . what if every child on earth was able to recognize and follow only the positive role models in his or her world. . .

6
You — A Miracle in the Middle of Happening

Few people stop to realize how miraculous they are. If you had a machine that could do all the things you can do, wouldn't you think it was amazing? You can move, breathe, think, learn, laugh, and talk. You are soft and sensitive at the same time you are flexible, strong, and durable. Why you're likely to last over a hundred years if you take care of yourself. What other thing on earth is as wondrous as a human being? And guess what? Somebody gave you one--a human being that is all your own to do with as you please. You've got one—it's YOU.

Now you may have ideas about your ears being too big or your nose too long; you may think you are too tall or too short, too wide or too thin. But whatever you may think—you are the ever so fortunate owner of one very remarkable piece of machinery.

Self-Esteem

We hear a lot of talk about self-esteem, which means valuing yourself, caring about yourself. You'd think self-esteem would come naturally, and maybe it does. In most cases, however, children learn pretty fast that they are loaded with faults. Parents, brothers and sisters, teachers, the rest of the world, including the media, start to tell them that they are not perfect. In fact, they learn that they make mistakes all the time, can't do what they're expected to do, and have looks that are not nearly as beautiful as the models and actors they see in the media. If they happen to believe all that negative feedback and if they receive little positive feedback, the result is low self-esteem. They don't value themselves anymore.

The trick is to learn how to hold on to your self-worth even when people and circumstances tell you differently. You make mistakes, you fail to meet the expectations of others, and you even let yourself down sometimes by doing something you really don't want to do. In spite of all this—and all of it happens to everybody—people with high self-esteem are able to hang on to their dignity. In other words, they forgive themselves, they tell themselves they will do better next time, and they quit trying to meet everyone else's expectations. They set their own goals and they meet them.

Here's how Nicky learned to maintain self-esteem:

When I was little I had trouble hanging out with girls. I was interested in what the boys were doing, like basketball and football. I liked to sit and watch them play and soon I was playing with them. If I had stayed much with girls I would have had low self-esteem because if a girl didn't have what they had—nice hair, clothes, etc.—they would consider her notches below them. All I ever liked to wear were jeans, sweatshirts, T-shirts, and sweatpants. I always thought a "real friend" wouldn't care what you wore. The girls would sting on me by calling me names like "Boldy Locks" and "Tom Boy." The boys, though, would accept me and tell me I was their best friend, invite me over to eat or play checkers or Connect Four—just silly games but fun. Eventually I had female friends, too, who could accept me the way I was.

Nicky as a little girl

I always kept my grades up. No matter what was on my mind, my schoolwork came first—then it was time to play. I was a bookworm and loved to read stories out loud, and when we had spelling bees I would often win. The teachers seemed to like me. In fact, I was often "teacher's pet." I liked the attention good grades and good attendance gave me. This helped me keep my self-esteem.

Because I was feeling good about myself, others seemed to look up to me. In 6th and 7th grade I was elected president of student council. I was still very popular when I entered high school, but then I started going down the wrong path, trying to get my self-esteem from gang banging.

Discussion Questions

1. People have different preferences in the things they like to do. Not so long ago, girls were not allowed to play rough sports, and boys weren't encouraged to cook or sew. Do you think there are certain activities that should be reserved for only boys or only girls?

2. Nicky says that because she felt good about herself, others looked up to her. Do you think this is a general truth? If you think well of yourself, will others think well of you, too? Explain why this could happen. What about the reverse—if you think poorly of yourself, will others think poorly of you?

3. Think about what it means to be "popular" in school. Why are some kids "popular" and others not? Can a person be popular for the wrong reasons, for example, for being rude to teachers and other students or for clowning around during class? What about for being in a dangerous gang?

Self-Esteem is a Two-way Street

It's sad to think about it, but other people can have a great deal of power over your self-esteem—if you let them. When you look or act the way they want you to, then they praise you and reward you. If you fail to do what they think you should be doing, then you get insults and complaints. But, think about it, you do the same thing to other people. You praise them for what you believe are good traits or actions and "dis" them for what you think are faults.

Nicky let people's opinions sway her when she got to high school, she stopped taking schoolwork seriously and she ended up in a gang because she thought she was doing the right thing.

I'm 26 years old and I am just now getting my GED. I started playing the clown in school, hanging out in the hallways, and my grades started dropping. The sad thing is my classmates still thought I was cool. They would laugh and cheer me on when I clowned around in class. I was still very popular the day I dropped out of school. People looked up to me because I was a good fighter and I was a member of the Bloods. Now that I am positive I'm even more loved and respected, but back then I didn't understand that this could happen.

I don't blame those who urged me on in the wrong direction. I blame myself. But later when I had been shot twice and had spent months in a jail cell, I knew that I had been confused about what is cool and what is not. Bullet wounds and prison are not cool.

Discussion Questions

1. Can you think of a time your friends encouraged you to do something that was not good for you? How did you respond? Why? How did you feel afterwards?

2. Do you think sometimes kids have difficulty deciding what is best for them? How can a person know what's the best thing to do, especially when friends are pushing them a direction they aren't sure they want to go? How do you make difficult decisions?

Getting back to YOU

People base their actions on their value system, which is simply what they believe to be valuable in their lives. If you truly value YOU and want to take care of YOU, you won't put yourself in danger, you won't do things that could ruin your future, things that could cause you great pain and suffering. Why? Because you love this human being too much to do her or him in with unwise decisions.

Nicky was valuing the opinions of her schoolmates over her own self. She was throwing away a high school diploma, and much worse, she was placing herself in great danger. The danger of being shot and killed or put away in prison for many years.

What can you do for yourself? Think of yourself as a fabulous machine that you want to keep in top-notch condition. What can you do right now that will maintain your physical health, your mental health?

Handling Criticism

Nicky ignored what the girls were saying about her and found new friends who liked her the way she was. What can you do to handle criticism that could threaten your self-esteem?

Below are some ideas others have had about handling criticism:

1. Listen carefully without interrupting.

2. Consider the comment information that you can accept or reject.

3. If you think they may be right, admit it and decide whether it is something about yourself you wish to change. If you think they may be wrong, tell them you appreciate the feedback and leave it at that. If it's something you can't change like height or race, then the criticism is definitely unjustified and should be removed from your mind immediately. Furthermore, the person giving this kind of destructive criticism is one to avoid as much as possible in the future.

4. Recognize that feedback, even negative feedback, can help people grow, but only if they add it to the many positive things they already know about themselves. Any negative comment is a good reason for reviewing all the positive things about you.

5. Don't dwell on the comment, especially if you decide it's right. Think of ways to improve and get on with your life. Always focus on your strengths, never your weaknesses.

Bobby G Learned to Love Himself Too Late

The following is a true story based on a news article and what Nicky knew about a boy from her neighborhood who was murdered in a drive-by shooting.

Bobby G was basically a good boy. All the time he was growing up he was good to his mother and dad and kind to his sisters. He was always a little small for his age and had been born with a learning disability, so people often thought he was younger than he really was. He struggled in school, but just never seemed to be able to get good grades. He really wanted to please his mother with a good report card.

When he got to high school, passed on by the school system without really learning the basics, his time in school became even more difficult. He couldn't read all the teachers wanted him to read and he couldn't do most of their assignments. Of course, he didn't ask for extra help. He was embarrassed and tried to hide his learning disability. He started to develop an "I don't care" attitude to cover up the fact that he really did care, but didn't know what to do about it.

About this time, several of his friends joined the Bloods. They pushed him to hang out with gang members and participate in things like drinking alcohol and smoking marijuana. It felt good to have a group to hang out with. This group didn't care if he couldn't do school work very well. Most of them couldn't either, and school was the last thing they wanted to be good at. Before he knew it, he was one of them, and he dropped out of school.

His mother was heartbroken because she knew what he was up to, though he never really told her. She knew he was running with a gang because he stayed out, sometimes all night long. She begged him to call her during the night, so she'd know he was still alive. He usually did call her because he loved his mother and didn't want her to worry about him.

He was now heavily involved in selling crack cocaine and carried a gun. He watched several homies, including a cousin, get shot down and killed by rivals. He was sick at heart, but he was also attached to the money he was making selling crack. He vowed in his heart that when he had earned enough money to get him started in a new direction, he would quit the gang life.

By this time he had a girlfriend and a baby son. One day, after barely escaping getting caught by the police, he decided to quit. He found a job and avoided his old homies who were still caught up in the gang. Unfortunately, he had angered rivals and he knew several of them were looking to kill him. He lived in fear every day, watching his back, being especially careful when he was with his family or girlfriend and baby. He really didn't want them to be hurt.

Rumors told him he was first on a hit list. He tried hard to show his mother, his girlfriend, and baby son, that he cared—telling them so and buying them gifts with money earned at his new job. He told his mother that someday she would be proud of him, yet in his heart he feared he wouldn't live another day.

But he had started to take care of himself too late. He had waited too long to get out of the gang. On a chilly winter night in 1998, a rival shot him in the head as he was leaving a friend's house. He died instantly. The Oregonian, *Portland's newspaper, stated that when police found his body, they found in his hand a photo of "his round-faced son smiling, showing off all four of his new front teeth."*

Though the police questioned everyone they could think of, they had no leads or suspects. No one seemed to know what had happened. Even today his murderer goes unpunished.

Discussion Questions

1. What do you think are some reasons why Bobby G. was caught up in the gang life?

2. Do you think he somehow knew he was going to be killed? If so, is there anything he could have done to save his life?

3. What do you think went wrong? Why was he killed even when he had made a major effort to stay away from gang life?

4. Why do you think the police have no suspects or witnesses? Do you think that some people may know who committed this murder but are too afraid to

speak up? Can you think of a way to protect witnesses, so that they will feel free to provide information to the police?

5. Do you think that people in the school system contributed in any way to Bobby G's involvement in gangs? What could they have done?

6. Can Bobby G's death help save the lives of other young people? How might this work? What could his mother, girlfriend, and friends do to help others understand the dangers of gang life? What would you do if you were one of them?

7. If you were Bobby G's girlfriend or mother, what would you tell Bobby G's son about his father when he was old enough to understand? How could you make him understand that his father was a good man, who cared about himself and others--but turned around too late to save his own life?

Activities

1. Write a letter to someone who has suffered the death of a loved one. What can you say to let them know you care that they are in pain?

2. Every time you meet a goal, your self-esteem goes up a bit higher. Make a list of goals each day that you want to accomplish, small goals that will be one baby step closer to your highest goals. As you meet each one, check it off on your list. You now have positive proof that you are progressing.

3. Think about the saying, "The best thing you can do for others is to take good care of yourself." In a short essay, explain how doing this would help 1) your family, 2) your friends, and 3) your community.

4. Pretend for a moment that you have been given a wonderful gift—a human being who is none other than you. Now what are you going to do with this gift? Love it? Take care of it? Use it to help others? Write an imaginary story telling what you are going to do to take care of this wonderful gift.

5. To accompany the story you wrote in exercise #4, create a collage of magazine pictures that illustrate what you will provide for your own special

human being. Place it on your bedroom wall where it will remind you every morning how valuable you are.

6. Set a timer for three minutes. Before the timer goes off, write as many positive things about yourself as you can think of. Try this activity several times, increasing the number of positive traits each time.

7. Do you have younger brothers and sisters, or younger cousins or friends? What can you do to help them value themselves? How can you help raise their self esteem? Brainstorm with your group, writing down ideas. Try some of them on the young people in your life. Report to the group on the results.

8. Write a newspaper article about Bobby G's death. Remember that a news article has a lead (first paragraph) that includes the who, what, where, why, and when of the event. Most important, remember that a news article can only report the facts. The writer can not insert his or her opinions or feelings.

9. Now write an editorial about Bobby G. An editorial is an opinion about a current event or person based on the writer's own ideas. This time you can include your own thoughts, feelings, and opinions. If your editorial is not specific to Bobby G, but gives your opinion about the gang situation and a possible solution, you could send it to your local newspaper as a letter to the editor. You might also send it to a government official.

10. An article in *The Wall Street Journal* entitled "Dealer Loses, A crack gang's accounting ledger says a lot about the economics of the drug business" on Monday, September 28, 1998, told the truth about the money kids in gangs make selling drugs. It may surprise you to discover that when the weekly income of a street drug seller was analyzed, it came to only $180.25 a week, just slightly above minimum wage. Not much pay for risking your life and your future. Find the article and report the details to your group.

Imagine. . . what if all young people were able to love themselves enough to take good care of themselves and keep themselves out of harm's way.

7
Pain:
Yours,
Mine,
Ours

People are always trying to remove pain from their lives. They take all manner of drugs, both legal and illegal; they bury themselves in television, movies, or books; they go to church; they go to bars; they go to doctors; and sadly they sometimes hurt other people or hurt themselves. But, no matter how hard people try, they cannot make themselves "painproof." Nobody gets through life without feeling pain—not the greatest athlete in the world, not the richest, the smartest, the best looking, or even the strongest person in the world. So what's a person to do?

Pain comes in two forms: emotional pain and physical pain. They are very closely related and often if you're feeling one or the other, it won't be long before you're feeling both. Many people think that physical pain must be the most difficult to handle—a toothache, a broken bone, a cut, a gunshot wound. However, they think this only until they experience some very difficult emotional pain—the death of a loved one or the loss of a lover or friend.

Nicky has felt much pain in her lifetime, especially when she was in the Bloods. Today she feels pain when she learns that another young person has been killed in a drive-by, but when she was in the gang, chances are the life taken would be that of a "homie," a close friend. She's been to more funerals than weddings, more hospital waiting rooms than graduation parties. She's been shot twice herself and has lost 24 friends to gang violence. Nicky knows about pain.

Physical pain can't always be avoided. Accidents happen. However, the physical pain Nicky felt when she was in the Bloods didn't have to happen—but it did.

"Taking Heat"

Nicky knows what it feels like to be shot. This is physical pain followed by lots of emotional pain. She tells below how "taking heat" feels:

The first time I got shot was in November of 1992. I thought that was my first and last time, but I was wrong. I was out with my homegirl, going to get burgers, when rivals just ran up on us shooting. I remember thinking at the time, "Oh, my god, I'm dead," wondering how many hot ones (shots) I could take before I died. As it turned out, I was shot only in the leg, but I learned what getting shot was like, and I knew I didn't want to take heat ever again for my homies or anybody. I knew then why they call a gun "heat." A bullet going into you is hot, burning hot.

Nicky just after she was shot the second time.

Just a year later I was with two homegirls, Treese and B. We stopped by my auntie's house to get something to eat. My auntie had been out of town for two weeks and today she was supposed to be back. I had been drinking and didn't want to be home with alcohol on my breath when she got back. I fixed a sandwich, cut it in three pieces, and went back out to the car just as my auntie and her boyfriend pulled up. We helped them unpack and then took off to the store to find my brother Slim. She didn't notice that I had been drinking. Now I wish she had noticed and had kept me from leaving the house.

We parked in the store parking lot where some of my homies were standing around on the corner. Then I noticed rivals driving by real slow. I started yelling, "Rivals must die" at the top of my lungs. My mind affected by the alcohol was not thinking clearly, and I thought I was being tough. Then I

Pain: Yours, Mine, Ours - 59

noticed the passenger in the front had his hand out the window, and then he started unloading on all of us standing there. Lucky, none of us was killed but I was shot in the buttocks and my cousin in the leg.

When I got out of the hospital the next day, my homies asked if I had watched the news, but I hadn't. Then they drove me by several houses belonging to the rivals. Those houses looked like Swiss cheese, full of holes. My heart sank because I knew one of them had a grandma in one of those houses. If my homies had killed their granny by accident, I feared for my own relatives who would be in danger from their retaliation. I learned later that no one was shot or killed, but this didn't take away my fear.

Today because of my gunshot wounds I have some pretty ugly scars and worse than that, I can't run or move as fast as I used to. Playing basketball and other sports is no longer an option. I'm not disabled but I'm not as good as I was before. I'm lucky I'm not dead.

After I got shot, it seemed my friends treated me differently. To me, it seemed like people acted as though they were scared when I came around. I don't know but maybe they were scared there were going to be shootings or fights happening. I could tell they didn't feel safe, and a lot of times I felt out of place and unhappy.

A lot of times friends would just sit and watch me. They couldn't keep a conversation or they'd rather not keep a conversation. I don't know if others have felt this way, but I could tell when people didn't feel safe around me. On top of this, I didn't want to jeopardize my family or friends. Gang life affects everyone around you. I don't care if they are your very best homies, they don't want to take a bullet for you. As my grandma says, "Bullets don't have no names."

Discussion Questions:

1. Nicky seems to find herself in the wrong place at the wrong time. What could she have done, if anything, to prevent what happened? What mistakes did she make? What could she have done instead?

60 - Ask Nicky

2. Nicky doesn't write much about the physical pain her wounds brought her. What emotional pain did the shootings bring?

3. How would you feel about being around someone who had been shot and might again be a target for gang members? What would you do if a friend of yours got shot while involved with gang activity?

4. Do you think Nicky learned something from the pain, both physical and emotional? What has she learned that maybe she didn't think about before?

Going to Jail

Nicky has been in jail three times as well as in a halfway house. Each time she learned a little more about herself, but she doesn't recommend jail to anyone. Jail is a very lonely place.

My first time going downtown to jail I didn't know what to expect, but "gangsta" or not I was shaking in my boots! My only ideas about jail had come from movies, and they made it look pretty bad. But I guess they didn't really scare me because I probably wouldn't have become so bad. So when I went to jail I was expecting to see bars sliding, no doors opening, and a bunch of women holding hands going through it all together. It didn't happen like that.

You are wakened about 5:30 a.m. everyday. Breakfast is served about 6. You might be able to go back to sleep for awhile, but by 8:30 your bed must be made and you must be dressed. You can't go back to bed again until after dinner. You are given exactly 15 minutes for each meal—yes, they actually time you. I remember the food as being horrible. You're very lucky if you can adjust to that food. The rest of the day drags. You might be able to watch TV in a circle-like environment, but you must be totally quiet while watching, or the TV goes off. You might play cards or dominoes.

The second time in jail I learned about "the hole," which is where they put you if you get into trouble. Trouble means you talked back to a guard, argued with an inmate, or were found with what they call "contraband," which is anything you're not supposed to have—could be as simple as an orange or an extra piece of clothing you didn't check in with. You can get a "trusty," which is a trusted inmate with special privileges to get you things you want. But if you get caught with it—it's the hole for you.

The hole is a small room in a long dark hall of 10 or 15 other small rooms just like it. When you walk into it, on the left is a toilet, on the right is your bunk with a small desk across from it. No windows. You are in the hole for 23 hours every day. You eat all three meals in there by yourself. They slide your food through a hole in the door.

I learned to like the hole because they let me have paper and pencil, and I could spend the day writing without interruption. There alone in that tiny dark place, I spent a lot of time thinking about my life, writing about it. I began to understand what I was doing wrong and began to plan how I could change.

Discussion Questions:

1. Nicky was sent to jail for selling drugs. Do you think jail is a good punishment for drug dealers? Why or why not? Can you think of other ways to handle people who commit crimes?

2. Jail was kind of like a long "time-out" for Nicky. Do you think it had a positive effect on her? Does "time-out " work in school or at home?

3. Why do you think it took three trips to jail for Nicky to change?

4. What do you think is the worst part about going to jail? Explain why.

5. Paper and pencil became tools for Nicky to understand herself. How could writing help you understand yourself? Have you ever used writing as a way to understand yourself better?

Get Tough!

No one can really avoid pain completely, but you can learn to handle it. You can also learn how to keep from hurting yourself. If you've learned to love yourself as a special human being, you will learn to avoid behaviors that will cause you pain.

When Nicky spent almost 20 days in the hole in jail, she was feeling extreme emotional pain. Unconsciously, she began to develop the steps listed on the following page. She wrote out her feelings. She wrote about all the events and behaviors that had led up to these feelings. She made a list of what she really wanted to do to change her life. This was the beginning of Nicky's turnaround. She gave up gang life and started writing the truth about it. She wanted to help others stay away from the physical and emotional pain negative gang activity brings.

As Nicky did, you can learn to toughen yourself emotionally, physically, and mentally. This doesn't mean that you grit your teeth and bear it. Instead, you can practice a healthy way of life that combats pain.

Physical Pain
Physical pain occurs when the body is injured through an accident or attacked by disease. An Olympic athlete was once severely injured in a car wreck. Most people would have died from the terrible injuries she received; however, she experienced complete recovery in a relatively short period of time. Her doctor, who was amazed, said the only reason she was able to recover so rapidly was the excellent physical condition she was in at the time of the accident.

If your body is healthy, it can take injury better and immediately start to heal. It is also better able to fight off colds, flu and other germs. So how can you keep yourself healthy? We bet you aleady know. There are four simple steps.

Eat good foods:
Sure cokes and french fries taste great, but they won't make you strong and healthy. You need plenty of fruits and vegetables, milk, grains and meats to build your body.

Get enough sleep:
If your body gets enough rest, it is able to handle daily stresses much better. Sleep is a time for growing and replenishing energy. A person with a rested mind and body moves better, thinks better, and feels good.

Pain: Yours, Mine, Ours - 63

Move that body:
Your body wants to move. It was made to move. So walk, run, jump, play, and dance. If you are a person with a disability, move whatever you can any way you can. Nicky can't play as hard as she used to before she was shot, but she still gets herself moving. Exercise makes your muscles and bones stronger and your skin and eyes bright.

Leave the poisons alone:
You may not think of alcohol, tobacco, and other drugs as poison, but, in fact, they are. The root word *tox* means poison. If you are intoxicated, you have poisoned yourself. Putting substances such as these into your body is like feeding yourself poison. You may not take enough to kill yourself, but any amount threatens the health of your body, making it more susceptible to disease and injury. This is in addition to the other kinds of trouble using drugs can cause.

Emotional Pain
Emotional pain is more complicated than physical pain. Living a healthy life will help, but no matter how good you live, emotional pain will find you. No one really escapes. Emotional pain has to be worked through. You have to consciously think through your pain. Nicky learned this when she was in "the hole" all by herself. Before she had cut off emotional pain, refusing to feel it and refusing to deal with it. Now she decided to face it and do something with it.

The steps on the next page make up Nicky's method of emotional pain control. Each one begins with a letter of her name, not to be cute and clever, but to help people remember the steps better. If you can remember how to spell Nicky, you can remember these steps.

Pain Can Be Contagious

Physical pain can lead to emotional pain; emotional pain can lead to physical pain. Your pain can cause me pain. Our pain can affect the whole community. That's why negative gang activity in any neighborhood hurts the whole community. The pain spreads in many ways.

Nicky's Method

Name exactly how you feel—sad, angry, hurt, ashamed, guilty. Then let yourself FEEL it without acting upon it. Write it down or tell somebody. But limit your description to **how** you feel, don't get into the **why** immediately.

Identify but don't judge. Identify the events or behaviors leading up to this feeling, but don't waste time trying to figure out who is to blame for the way you feel. Even if you, yourself, are the problem, don't judge yourself. What happened has happened. Accept it and look for the next step.

Create a list of things you can do right now to make things better--not just for yourself, but for everyone involved.

Kick-start yourself to do something right now.

Yes, you can do it! With a positive attitude you can turn things around and begin to make changes in your life.

Activities

1. Keep a journal that records your experience in following Nicky's steps for dealing with emotional pain. Write three parts: 1) describe the event that has caused pain, 2) tell how you used Nicky's method, 3) describe the results. Did the method help?

Pain: Yours, Mine, Ours - 65

2. The media tend to tell us that every pain has a drug, over-the-counter or prescription, to make it go away. Watch television and look through the ads in magazines and newspapers. Make a list of the kinds of advertisements you find that claim they can handle pain.
Discuss in your group if this is a problem in our society. Do children grow up thinking that there is a drug for every pain they encounter? Why is this a problem?

3. Imagine a life in which you had no feeling. You were unable to feel pain or pleasure of any kind, somewhat like the androids in science fiction films. What would life be like? Write a story about living with no feeling. Afterwards, discuss the following questions in your group: 1) Is pain actually a good thing in some ways? 2) Would people get along better if no one had feelings? 3) What problems would we have in our society if no one could feel anything?

4. A controversial issue in our society today is whether doctors should help people who have incurable illnesses and are suffering great pain to commit suicide. Do you think this is a good policy? Discuss it in your group. Make a chart of the pros and cons of the issue.

5. Psychologists tell us that crying is an excellent release for emotional pain for both men and women. Discuss crying in your group. Consider the following questions: 1) Is crying only acceptable for females, or is it a human thing, something both males and females do on occasion, 2) Why do people cry at weddings and graduations? How can a happy event stimulate tears?

6. Research the nervous system. Why do people feel pain? How does the body know it has been emotionally hurt when there is no visible injury to a particular part of the body. Pain is a brain function. Why then do people speak of emotional pain as affecting the heart, breaking it? You may want to interview a physician for this information. Report your findings to the group.

*Imagine . . . what if people learned how to keep
from bringing pain on themselves and others
and how to make themselves tough enough to
handle the pain that cannot be avoided. . .
what if they learned how to make their bodies,
minds and hearts strong.*

8
Peace . . .
It Starts with You

> *Violent gang members all over the country are tired—tired of watching their backs, tired of pretending to be tough, tired of keeping a gun, tired of lying to their families— but how can it all end? This one is killed in retaliation for that one, who was killed in retaliation for another, and on and on. The body count gets larger, more hearts and dreams are broken and destroyed, and more tears are shed.*
> *Elie Wiesel, (pronounced LE Vzel) survived a concentration camp in World War II. His writings about nonviolence have been read around the world. He says, "Who ever kills, kills his brother." He doesn't talk about people wearing red or blue, about dark skins or white skins. He believes everyone is your brother or sister. You and every other person are part of the whole family of human beings. When one individual is hurt or destroyed, the whole family suffers. Your behavior affects the whole human family; you can help or you can hurt.*
> *It starts with you.*

It takes courage to walk away from a gang. Gang members are a tight group. They don't talk to others outside the gang about their activities. They keep their mouths shut even when what they know could save the life of someone else. Police complain about their inability to get any information about the shooter after a gang shooting. Everyone involved clams up, perhaps out of gang loyalty but mostly out of fear. Retaliation is a real threat. No one wants to get hurt or killed for speaking out.

In early 1997, Nicky started speaking out. She was tired of watching people she cared about die. She herself had already suffered two gunshot wounds, one made her fear she might not walk again. She'd just spent 20 days in "the hole" in the county jail, thinking and writing. Now she wanted to change. Before she had been a leader for others in violent gang activities; now she wanted to lead the other direction.

Nicky writes about "Getting Out"

It all started in 1997. I realized it was time to get "down and dirty," which means to get serious about something. It was time for me to quit thinking just about myself and start thinking about others, to care about others even when they don't care about themselves. I didn't want to abandon my friends. I wanted to turn them around in the direction I was going—away from violence, breaking the law, playing the gang game. And not just the side I was from, the Bloods, but the other side, too—no matter how hard-headed they might be or how they might act towards me.

Nicky and her good friend Portland Police Officer, Victoria Wade.

One month after I started working and talking against gangs, I was contacted by Channel 6, a local television station. They wanted me to tell them all about girls in gangs because they wanted to do a three-day special called Girl Gangsta's. And so I did. I told them what I knew, talking live on camera. The reporter and I cruised through the neighborhood, and on camera I talked about the gang shootings I had been part of. Nobody in or out of Portland gangs had ever done such a thing.

I called in some of my younger "deuces," girls who looked to me as a leader. I don't know what happened. They were supposed to be themselves, but once they got in front of that television camera, they started "showing out," which means they were acting like gang members. They'd never been on television before, and I guess they wanted to look tough. They started hitting up gang signs and speaking gang talk. They even spotted some rivals on the street as we were cruising in the neighborhood. One said, "Get them rivals on camera because that's the last time you'll see them." And so the Channel 6 camera did.

When asked what they would do if rivals killed one of their homies, one said, "If they shoot or kill one of my homies, we will kill one or two of theirs." All of this was on camera for the whole community to watch on the nightly news.

Five days later the police kicked down the door of one of the houses we had spotted and took all five occupants to jail. They found drugs inside the house.

Now the hood could have "dissed' me and called me a "snitch," and some of them did, but I found that many would still smile and wave, nod their heads, and say, "Keep on truckin', Nicky." Some of my old homie "friends" talk bad about me because I have changed. But I know that if I was still on the corner selling dope and hittin' up signs, they'd still be in my face. It took me long enough to realize that I had to change my friends, my attitude and my dress code and do something positive with my life.

Discussion Questions:

1. Why do you think Nicky's "deuces" reverted to gang behavior, knowing that Nicky had turned against gangs? Do you think people might act different in front of a camera than they do normally? Why or why not?

2. This news show was responsible for five people getting caught with drugs. How would you feel if you were Nicky or one of her deuces? Explain.

3. Do you think that if Nicky had not decided to leave the gang life, she would have consented to doing this news show? Why are gang members so reluctant to speak out? What would happen if they all did?

4. Different people in Nicky's neighborhood responded to her in different ways after she quit banging. Who do you think might support her and who might not? Do you think that some gang members might have been glad that she had spoken out? Why?

5. After Nicky left the gang, some people talked badly about her, but no one on either side tried to hurt her physically. Why do you think they didn't make her house their next drive-by?

Walk on the Side of Peace

Walk in the footsteps of people like Dr. Martin Luther King Jr.; Gandhi of India; Chief Joseph, a Native American; Rev. Tutu of South Africa; Princess Diana of England and others like them but who may not have their names in history books. In the midst of conflict, they were willing to take the side of peace and speak out against violence and discrimination. We look at them as heroes, but anyone of us could do the same. Nicky is a hero because in her community that was tormented by gang murders and crime, she was willing to remove herself from gang affiliation and speak out against violence, determined to help young people stay out of harmful gangs.

Sometimes people mistakenly think that being on the side of peace means letting other people walk over you and treat you badly without responding. That's not the way it works. Would people who had decided to value and love themselves let others hurt them? No way. Martin Luther King Jr. said, "Get angry, but don't get violent."

When people are injured or treated unfairly, they generally respond in three different ways: submissively, confidently, or violently.

Submissive:
Submissive people do not value themselves. In fact, others' needs and desires are always put first. They avoid stating their needs, feelings, and opinions, and cannot make decisions. They are weak and afraid.

Confident:
Self-confident people respect both their own needs as well as those of others. They speak and act directly, honestly, and sincerely, and they take

responsibility for their actions.

Violent:

Violent people do not respect the rights of others. They are argumentative, mean, selfish, and hurtful. They always want to be in control. They use threats and physical and verbal abuse to get their way.

	What it looks like	How they feel	How others feel	What happens
Submissive	No eye contact Poor posture Mumbling Keeps busy to avoid subject	Angry inside Taken for granted Resentful Feelings are hurt Guilty	Frustration Pity Try to avoid Realize they can take advantage and do	Submissive person is rolled over, taken advantage of
Confident	Good eye contact Relaxed posture Easy tone of voice, loud enough, but not too loud	Self-respectful Secure High self-esteem Calm	Respected Understood Trustful May be frustrated if unable to get own way	Confident per- son is likely to get needs met; if not, he or she feels good about self; often prob- lem is resolved.
Violent	Tense, excited Tight muscles Loud voice Violent actions Finger pointing Harsh words	Self righteous Important Powerful Sometimes guilty Sometimes lonely	Hurt, angry Embarrassed Wants revenge Afraid Resentful Tries to avoid	Conflict is worsened Both sides feel angry. No problems resolved People are hurt Bad feelings

Look at the chart above to see how each kind of behavior makes a person feel, how other people feel about the person acting that way, and what is accomplished.

Gandhi said, "An eye for an eye will leave the whole world blind."

Discussion Questions:

1. Think of times when you acted each of the three ways—one when you were submissive, one when you were confident and another when you were violent. What was the result each time? Could you have handled the situation better had you chosen to walk on the side of peace?

2. How do you usually respond when someone acts violently towards you? Are there better ways of responding?

3. Eleanor Roosevelt, the wife of the former U.S. President Franklin D. Roosevelt once said, "No one can make you feel inferior without your consent." What do you think she meant and how does it relate to the chart?

Nicky says, "It's better to walk in peace than 'rest in peace.'"

It was hard for Nicky to face all her old homies and tell them she wasn't going to be part of their gang activity anymore. She confidently told them she didn't want to be involved with any more violence or killing. She still lives in her same neighborhood today, but she walks on the side of peace.

There's much more to it than just killing one another. Sometimes homies are killing others to get attention, to make themselves feel more important—and it's not just in a gang environment. Violence is happening among young people all over, even when they aren't in a gang. They kill in jealousy, anger, revenge, but it all boils down to not being happy with themselves.

All you have to do is believe in yourself. Sometimes that's hard, so it helps to find someone you trust to talk to. When you're feeling bad about something, it's a relief to be able to tell someone, so you don't have to keep so much to yourself. Believe me I know it hurts more to keep things inside. I used to have a problem in that I never wanted to talk to anyone about how I really felt. I felt I couldn't trust anyone. Then I found out that my grandma was there for me even when I had done wrong. She listened and loved me anyway. I always remember her saying, "Only God can judge you."

If you can't find someone to talk to, you can talk to me by email or letter. I

Peace. . . It Starts with You - 73

will try to understand, and I promise I won't judge.

Don't feel that you are a "sucka" if you walk away from a fight. To me, it only proves that you have decided that life is too precious to risk it over a foolish argument. I want to say to my "Ol Skool Homies," who don't bang anymore, "Congratulations!" And to all the young people who tell me "I quit because I have too much to look forward to," I give you two thumbs up! Don't let anyone or anything turn you around. Stay strong. I know it's not that easy— easier said than done.

Instead of going to the corner to sling dope and throw up gang symbols, trying to become another statistic, do something positive. When I'm feeling sad, I write or go and sit with my grandma. Sometimes I go to the cemetery and just sit and reminisce about the friends I've lost, the good times I had with them, and how easily we lost them over something stupid.

Discussion Questions:

1. Once a person is on the right track, staying away from gang activity, how can he or she stay on that track? What can you suggest?

2. What do you think Nicky means when she says, "All you have to do is believe in yourself"? Can you give some ways of developing a belief in yourself? You might think back to Unit 6 on self-esteem.

3. Judging can do a lot of harm to those on both sides. Sometimes you have to judge behavior, but what about the person? Can you give him or her another chance?

4. Nicky writes stories or goes to visit her grandmother or her friends' graves. What are some positive things you could do when tempted towards violent behavior?

Activities

1. Read about Martin Luther King Jr., Elie Wiesel, Gandhi, Chief Joseph, Rev. Tutu, Princess Diana, or another person known to be a peacemaker. Write

about them and share their stories with your group.

2. Keep a "Peace Journal" in which each day, you write about how you have been able to walk in peace, what you have done to avoid or stop violence. Share it every now and then with your group.

3. Police officers are often called peace officers. Interview a police officer focusing on how he or she works to maintain peace in the community. Tell your group about the interview.

4. Cut several articles out of the paper that are about violent happenings. Bring them to your group and discuss how that violent incident could have been avoided, why it happened, and what the community could do to see that it never happens again.

5. Form a peace club, give it a name, and brainstorm ways that you as a group could promote peace in your neighborhood. This might include writing letters to political leaders, posting peaceful signs and posters in the neighborhood, holding peace rallies, forming a conflict resolution action team to teach others, perhaps those in elementary school or in your own school or community, how to resolve their differences peacefully.

6. Find a problem in your neighborhood that is caused by violence and illegal activities, such as drug abuse, homeless teens, families hurt by gang activity, guns, and graffiti, and work to raise money to help stop it or volunteer to help in other ways.

Imagine . . . what if people around the world adopted peace as their motto and began to work towards peaceful relationships. . . what if your neighborhood or city did. . . what if you did?

9 Dreams Give You Wings

Can you think of anyone who is completely happy with his or her life the way it is? Some people may say so, but if you stop to talk to them about their lives, you find that no life is perfect; there is always something that would make it better.

Bill Gates, Microsoft billionaire and the richest person in the country, still has dreams about improving things in his business and in his personal life, and he works on them daily. Oprah Winfrey has the most popular talk show on television; she's beautiful, smart, and wealthy. Does she still have dreams? You bet. She's busy right now getting people to read good books and do good works. Her new endeavor is to help people change their lives and fulfill their dreams.

Do you have dreams? Have you ever shared them with someone, or are you a little embarrassed about them, afraid someone might think you are foolish? Don't give up on your dreams. In fact, think about them everyday and begin to figure out the steps that will make them come true. Dreams give you wings to fly out of any situation and begin something new and better.

Almost every accomplishment began with a dream. Mark McGwire and Sammy Sosa used to dream about breaking the home run record . . . and now they have. Oprah used to dream about having a television talk show . . . and now she does. Look around you: dreams are coming true everywhere you look. The woman who just opened the restaurant on the corner used to dream about having her own restaurant. The new teacher in your school used to dream about being a teacher. Someday when your dream comes true, you'll think, "I used to dream about doing this, and now I am doing it!"

Dreams Can Come True

James Todd Smith, whom you probably know better as **LL Cool J**, the popular rap singer, grew up in a tough area in New York City. Crime and violence were all around him, even in his own home. When he was only a child his father shot his mother in the back and his grandmother in the stomach. Later he became a juvenile delinquent, always in trouble. But from the time he was nine years old, he wrote rap lyrics, and though he still kept getting in trouble, he kept writing and making music, too. When he was 14, because he was out of control, his mother sent him to live with his father in Los Angeles. She had dropped the charges against him for shooting her and her mother.

It took a long time, but eventually James fulfilled the dreams he'd been dreaming all along. He became a successful rap artist—two Grammys, seven platinum albums, a television show and movie roles—but, even more important, he also became a husband and a father and developed the kind of family he had always longed for.

Morgan Freeman, Academy award nominee who has acted in dozens of outstanding films, started dreaming when he was a small child in Greenwood, Mississippi. He showed a natural talent for acting even when he was a small boy. Whenever he had an opportunity he would act out a part. His family and teachers encouraged him. He continued acting every chance he got, through high school and on to Hollywood where he persistently presented himself to the motion picture studios even though nobody had ever heard of him.

One disappointment followed another until he was given a role in the children's TV show *The Electric Company*. That was the beginning of a string of roles leading up to his prominence as a Hollywood actor today. Along the way he almost died of pneumonia, he had to fight and win a hard battle with alcohol, and he spent countless hours walking the streets looking for work, hungry and depressed. Success always seemed to be around the next corner, never in hand. But he didn't give up his dream of becoming an actor. Now you've seen him in excellent films such as *Driving Miss Daisy* and *Deep Impact*, in which he played the future President of the U.S.

Discussion Questions:

1. How are Morgan Freeman and LL Cool J alike? What characteristics do they share, and how did they put them to use to better their lives?

2. What hardships did each have to face before becoming successful?

3. Reread each story and tell what you can learn from their histories?

4. Do you know of other people, famous or not, who had a dream and kept working towards it until they reached it in spite of set-backs along the way? Tell about them.

Small Steps to Major Leaps

Dreams have to start somewhere—from daydreaming in your bed to watching a favorite performer, reading a book, listening to a song, or just thinking about something someone said. Dreams always have a set of steps that lead to them like a long staircase to the stars. People who finally make it to the stars have traveled a long way, one step at a time.

Passing a math test in middle school or taking a part-time job in high school may seem to be a long way from your dreams, but, in fact, they may be important steps along the way. Every day is another opportunity to work on your dreams.

Look at the chart on the next page that shows how a set of steps can lead to accomplishing a dream. Sometimes one step has a bunch of steps under it, so we have steps and sub-steps. Some are so small you might call them"baby steps," but, no matter how small, if aimed directly at your goal, each step is an important piece of the dream building.

Often dreams are attached to your own special talents, things you can do well and love to do. Nicky loves to write, LL Cool J loves to compose songs, and rap, while Morgan Freeman loves to act. When you recognize something you can do well, whether it's getting along with people, working math problems, playing football, modeling clothes, or one of a million other things, it

Step by step, you can reach your dream.

Dream:
"I want to become a defense attorney."

Steps to Fulfillment:
1. Working hard in school to perfect reading, writing, and speaking skills.
2. Graduation from high school with good grades.
>   Homework completed
>   Paying attention in class
>   Getting help with difficult subjects
>   Attending everyday
3. Getting a job to earn money
4. Saving money for school
4. Applying for scholarships and student loan programs
5. Getting an internship or volunteer job in a law office
6. Getting into college, taking pre-law courses
7. Working hard, passing college courses
8. Applying to law school
9. Applying for grants, scholarships, and student loans for law school
10. Studying hard, passing law classes
11. Studying for the bar exam
12. Passing the bar exam
13. Taking a job as an attorney

might just be something to hang a dream on. No one thinks about a talkative child becoming a talk show host or a 6th grader who likes to draw airplanes becoming an aviation engineer--but it can happen.

Make a list of all the good qualities and skills that you may have at this time. Keep in mind that you are not anywhere near finished collecting good qualities and skills. But what do you have right now? Get your friends and family to help with this list because sometimes it's difficult to recognize your own good qualities. Don't overlook things like "friendly," "good with animals," "good at growing plants," or things like "strong back and legs" and "nice smile." These traits that seem so minor may turn out to be the key to your success.

Good Qualities and Skills to Hang a Dream On	
Skill or Quality	How I can use it

Sometimes dreams arise when things seem wrong in your life. If you don't like living in a gang troubled neighborhood, you may dream about living somewhere else or about cleaning up the gang activity. If you don't like taking the bus everywhere you go, you may dream about owning a car. If you don't like being as thin as you are or as large as you are, you might dream about losing or gaining weight, building muscle, looking great in your clothes. If you have trouble reading, writing or doing math problems, you might dream of doing better in these things.

Make a list of the things in your life you'd like to change. They may turn into dreams worth developing.

Things in Your life You Want to Change

Whatever your dreams are, continue to nourish them and cherish them, because without a dream, nothing changes, and nothing gets better.

Dreams May Change Over Time—Don't Fret

As we grow older, gain new information about the world or about ourselves, sometimes dreams change. Here are some examples:

Andy dreamed of becoming a marine scientist working with whales and dolphins, but after visiting a marine laboratory, he saw that most of the scientists spent their time looking in microscopes and writing reports. Later he changed his dream to animal trainer. He wanted to actually work with the dolphins and whales, teaching them tricks and taking care of them.

Juanita dreamed of working in an office as her mother did. She liked organizing, filing, working on the computer, and answering the phones. When she was in high school she got an after-school job working in an office. She discovered that long hours in an office could be unexciting. She found herself wanting to go outside, talk to new people, and get away from a computer screen. After awhile she found another dream—a job as sales representative in which she could travel from client to client. This job would still include some office work—organization, filing, some computer work, and much telephoning-- only from a cell phone.

You are the only one who can change your dream. Don't let other people determine or destroy your dreams. **Mariah Taylor** grew up in Portland, Oregon. When she was in high school, her dream was to become a registered nurse. She told her high school counselor her dream, who looked very worried and said, "Mariah, I don't think you should think about becoming a nurse. Your math grades aren't that high. Why don't you consider becoming a nurse's aide?" Mariah wouldn't listen to this plan, but she did pay attention to what she said about her math skills. She went right out and found someone to help her better her math skills. She worked hard and learned well. Eventually, she entered college, earned her nursing degree and went on to become a nurse practitioner, the highest level of nursing, just below a doctor. Later, she opened her own medical clinic in her old neighborhood.

When you run into a wall in pursuing your dream, if you really want it bad enough, you will find a way to get around or over that wall. It all depends on your own determination.

Research on People Who Fulfill Their Dreams

Once a group of researchers decided to study a set of people who had all achieved their dreams. They wanted to find out if these people had any particular traits in common. They discovered that every one of them had five special abilities. These are abilities that others can model and develop. Successful people were . . .

Visionary

This means they could dream. They could see into the future and envision themselves accomplishing their dreams. They had a clear picture in their minds of what they wanted to do and be.

Confident

They believed in themselves and were confident that they could learn what they needed to learn and do what they needed to do to make their dream come true. They loved themselves and valued themselves and became their own best friends and supporters.

Courageous

If they knew they lacked skills in an important area needed to accomplish their dream, they weren't afraid to find help in learning that skill, to watch other people, to take classes and try hard. If they failed the first time, they tried again and again until they learned it, or they redesigned their dream. They weren't afraid of other people because they knew that they themselves were as valuable to the world as anyone else was, and that they had a great deal to offer.

Optimistic

Even when things went wrong, they were able to pick up with what was left and make good use of the experience. They had an amazing ability to see the good hiding inside the bad. For example, when Nicky's grandmother had to have her toe amputated, she saw that now the pain would be gone and she could wear the shoes she hadn't been able to wear for a long time. She saw the good hiding within the bad. When Nicky was sent to "the hole" in the county jail, she realized that now she would have plenty of time all by herself to do her writing and thinking. For the first time in her life, she was able to see her life clearly and plan changes.

Patient

They realized that success wouldn't arrive overnight, that it would take a good deal of planning and work. They didn't get discouraged when they looked at the large number of smaller steps they would have to take to reach their dreams. They just took one step at a time, redid steps when they had to, and kept on. They also knew that time and experience might show that the dream must be modified in some way. They had the patience and wisdom to redirect their path slightly or in some cases, remodel their dreams, but always their action was based on their own decision. No one else was in charge of their lives or their dreams.

In your group, design a poster that illustrates the traits of people who fulfill their dreams. Display it in your classroom as a reminder to everyone.

<u>Nicky has a Dream</u>

From the time I was a small child I wanted to be a teacher. I liked the idea of being the leader, but what I liked more was helping out as much as I could. The teacher used to let me do roll call and I was on Student Council when I was in 6th and 7th grade. I had to keep my grades and attendance up, but I liked being involved in planning for my classmates.

Even when I was a "gangsta" I always wanted to do something important for the community. I feel bad that I took people away from positive role models. They looked up to me and became negative. So since many of them still look up to me, I want to put something back into the community by being a positive role model.

I've seen too much and heard too much, and sometimes I think I'm going crazy in this neighborhood when I see people who are still banging. I'm out there trying to tell my homies, "Give it up!" I've got all kinds of ideas to help my homies and rivals, too. I want to see a big change in their lives as I have in mine. I want to have meetings and get the parents' attention.

In the beginning when I first started to change, I felt like I was all alone. The only person I had and could believe and count on was God, because so many people didn't believe I was ready to change. I didn't have too many people who acted like they were going to stand by my side. That was a letdown, and I could have turned to gangs again. Yes, I could have started back slinging dope and banging on the corners again, but I believed in myself and I knew not to give up because I didn't want to upset the handful that did believe in me. I had made up my mind a few years before that I was going to become a writer.

I am still interested in being a teacher or a youth counselor as well as a writer. The youth today feel like they can't trust anyone, so I want to be there for them. This book is the beginning of the fulfillment of my dreams. Someday I want to be able to say that yes, I am a writer, yes, I am a counselor to youth, and, yes, I am doing something for the community.

I blame myself for the deaths of some of my homies. If they had not looked up to me and followed me, some would be alive today. I came to believe that it was up to me to make the change first since I have had so many chances. I am a survivor, been shot two too many times, been to jail, and now I want to show them there is a way out of the Hood and not just six feet under or behind bars. If we all try, there is a way.

Dreams do come true as long as you believe in them and don't give up for anything or anyone.

Discussion Questions:

1. Do you think that many gang members give up trying to change? What discourages them? What do they need to turn around? How can the community provide what they need?

2. Nicky said she felt like she was all alone when she first started to change. Do you think that changing might be an "all alone" thing? Many people can guide you and believe in you, but is it really up to you? Why or why not?

3. Many things are motivating Nicky to change. What are her motivations, the reasons she wants to become positive instead of negative?

4. What can you do to help yourself and in turn help the community? Do you have a dream?

You have a Dream, too.

Think of your ultimate dream right now. What is a dream you carry deep in your heart, something that you really want? There may be many things that you dream of, but choose one right now that is special in some way.

Write about it. Describe it in detail because, remember, you must be able to see it in your mind before you can believe in it and accomplish it.

My Dream: _____

_____

_____

List the big steps that you must take to reach that dream. Each of these will probably have sub-steps that lead to their completion, but right now write down only the ones that come to mind. You may have many, many steps to reach before you see your dream come true. In fact, there may be steps you don't even know about now. Nevertheless, write down as many steps as you can see at this stage of your life. You might get your group members or your parent or teacher to help figure out the steps.

Steps Leading to My Dream:

1. _____

2. _____

3. _____

4. _____

86 - *Ask Nicky*

5. _____

6. _____

7. _____

8. _____

9. _____

10._____

Next think about the small steps you could be working on TODAY. What could you do today that would be a small step in the direction of fulfilling your dream? Write them below.

1. _____

2. _____

3. _____

4. _____

Everyday spend some time working on your dream. It might be getting your homework done; it might be practicing your ice skating or basketball technique; it might be as simple as eating right and getting enough sleep. Every step counts.

Guess what? If you've already designed a dream and started thinking about how to get there, you've already taken the first step in fulfilling your dream. Now hang onto it and don't let go.

One more thing. . .

*Imagine . . . that you have been given a
miraculous power to pursue your dreams. All you
must promise is to choose the positive path, the one
that will help you and your community.
Once your heart is set on a positive dream,
that power will energize and guide you to your
dream's fulfillment . . .if you can imagine this,
imagination will turn to reality.
Ask Nicky.*

Special Thanks from Nicky:

To God, all mighty, to my mom Enola and daddy Alvin for having me and supporting me.

To my four brothers: Slim, Boomer, Lil' Smack, and Scandless. I love you so much for your support.

To my two sisters who are so funny, RoRo and Saqoya, and step mom

To Sandra, you stay sweet and keep that pretty smile

To Giane Taylor, MooMoo, and Drina, this book is especially for you so you don't follow in my negative old ways.

To my Auntie Marsha and Jackie Robinson

To Uncle Dave, Chris, and Aundrae, I got so much love for you three.

To the Chaney family--Uncle Michael Chaney, you quit being so silly and thanks so much for your family support. You and your wife stuck by me and are still there.

To my homeboys and homegirls, Tanya and my Lil' Y.G., Keekee, stay sweet. Daelynn told you I was going to make it! Stay strong KeeKee, Saquoya, Vance. Keep on moving with a smile.

To Shena, Ciela, Lil' Damaria, Lil Scratch and Baby Scratch, all my relatives.

To Pooch--time is running out, you better stay strong.

To Grandma Minnie Black, much love. Grandpa Lawson, I'm doing it--being positive--thanks to you and Grandma

To Mama Karen Robinson, you kept your promise and I'm still here, thanks to your positive pushing.

To "K"Zell Wesson, you keep on slam dunkin' and shooting those 3 pointers with a smile.

To my homeboys, rappin' nationwide, You finally put P-Town on the map. Maniak Lok, Cool Nutz, and Kenny Mizzak Mack. I'm next for the map, you already know.

To RedRum we go way back. I got much love

To my "Ol' School Homies" in the pen, I haven't forgotten about any of you.

To those in the community who supported me, thank you. If not, you have your reasons.

Rest in peace, all my homies who are no longer here. I haven't forgotten you.

Love,

Nicky

Training for Parents and Educators

A 4-hour training is available for schools, agencies, and parent groups desiring more information and assistance in dealing with gang-affected and at-risk youth. Both Nicole Taylor and Frances Caldwell will be your trainers. Our training agenda is as follows:

Part 1 Overview
       Characteristics of troubled youth
       What works: 10 strategies that will help
       Q&A on gang behavior

Part 2 How to Make the Ask Nicky Program Work for You
       Ways to modify and expand the program
       Group management strategies

Part 3 Demonstration with Group of Teens
       You provide 5-10 young people
       We'll do a demonstration session with analysis following

> For more information or to schedule a training, call 1-877-262-5609. Training is free with an order of 50 or more books when expenses are paid.

The Ask Nicky Email Program

All emails with questions or comments on the Ask Nicky program are welcome and will be answered at no charge. Address these to books@aywnpublications.com.

Young people who wish a personal correspondence with Nicky may order an Ask Nicky Email Subscription. The first five emails to Nicky at nicky@aywnpublications.com with her personal response are free. Additional emails are charged on the following basis:

10 personal email letters from Nicky $25
20 personal email letters from Nicky $45
40 personal email letters from Nicky $75

To order an Ask Nicky Email Subscription:

Name_____

Affiliation _____

Address _____

City_____State____Zip_____

Phone _____

Fax # _____
Email _____

Method of Payment;

Check (make payable to AYWN Publications) ☐

MasterCard ☐ Visa ☐

Name_____

Card # _____

Expiration Date _____

Signature _____

Order additional books from **AYWN Publications**
2711 NW St. Helen's Road
Portland, OR 97210

To place credit card orders, call toll-free **1-877-262-5609**
or fax your order to us at **1-503-227-7470**
Visit us at www.aywnpublications.com

Please deliver to:

Name_____

Affiliation _____
(school, church, agency, business)

Address _____

City_____State____Zip_____

Phone _____

Fax # _____

Email _____

Method of Payment;

☐ Check (make payable to AYWN Publications)

☐ MasterCard   ☐ Visa

Name_____

Card # _____

Expiration Date _____

Signature _____

Title	Quantity	Price	Total Price
Ask Nicky. . . A Young Person's Workbook for Building Dreams			
Parent-Teacher Edition		$24.95	
Student Edition		$14.95	
		Sub-total	
Shipping & Handling (greater of 10% or $3.50)			
		Total Enclosed	

Available soon:

☐ **Ask Nicky Again**
Additional activities
and lessons for use
with teens

☐ **Nicky – Ex-Girl Gangsta'**
Nicky's complete autobiography as
a member of the Bloods; strong
prevention theme, written for
teens

☐ **The Last-Ditch Writing Book**
A workbook that uses a radical
new method of learning to write;
developed by a writing teacher
with over 25 years experience;
ideal for those who have failed in
the traditional writing class; also
works for ESL students.

Please notify me when these become available ☐